Breaking Open the Gospel of Matthew

Gerard P. Weber and Robert L. Miller

Breaking Open
the Gospel of Matthew

The Sermon on the Mount

ST. ANTHONY MESSENGER PRESS

Cincinnati, Ohio

Nihil Obstat: Rev. Arthur J. Espelage, O.F.M.
Rev. Edward J. Gratsch

Imprimi Potest: Rev. John Bok, O.F.M.
Provincial

Imprimatur: +Most Rev. Carl K. Moeddel, V.G.
Archdiocese of Cincinnati
November 24, 1997

The *nihil obstat* and *imprimatur* are a declaration that a book is considered
to be free from doctrinal or moral error. It is not implied that those who
have granted the nihil obstat and imprimatur agree with the contents,
opinions or statements expressed.

Cover and book design by Julie Lonneman
Illustration by Stephen D. Kroeger and Julie Lonneman
Electronic format and pagination by Sandy L. Digman

ISBN 0-86716-320-8

Contents

Introduction

WOULD YOU LIKE A MESSAGE of hope and assurance in this confusing world—along with some helps for a better, more peaceful life? If so, come along with us as we conduct an imaginary interview with the man who wrote the Gospel According to Matthew. We're going to ask a lot of questions about portions of his text in order to surface the basic attitudes toward life that lie behind the sermons and doings of Jesus, the Christ.

We are not going to do a scholarly work of interpreting the texts. Plenty of other books have done that. This book contains ideas and reflections that we trust will offer you hope and perhaps a different slant on life.

To make clear what is in our minds, we had better explain what we mean by attitudes. Attitudes lie behind everything we do. They are the motivators that prompt us to act in one way or another. Sometimes they are easy to identify. At other times they need to be dug out of their hiding places deep in our psyche.

Attitudes are complex. They are made up of our ideas, our perception and interpretation of events, as well as our feelings and our past experiences. Attitudes can be good or bad, positive or negative, helpful or harmful. The attitudes that motivated Jesus and are embedded in his sayings are the only ones that offer hope in a confused world and lead to growth and happiness. Therefore, we frequently need to examine our attitudes and give them a reality check. If any part of an attitude is out of touch with the truth as embodied in Jesus, it will lead us to act in ways that stunt our growth and dampen our happiness.

Perhaps a simple example of how attitudes influence our actions will help you understand what this book is about. Imagine that you are walking in a wooded area. Under a bush you see a thick spotted coil. It looks like a snake. You fear snakes: They are dangerous. You pick up a thick branch to bash its head—only to discover when you hit it that it is a coiled piece of rope. Your fear twisted your perception and prompted you to a rash and foolish act.

If you are to avoid making the same mistake a second time, your fear of snakes as well as your perception of what is really a snake needs a reality check. Not all snakes are dangerous; some are helpful. You need to learn how to distinguish the helpful from the harmful, to learn when your fear is justified and when it is not. Then you can make a wise decision about how to act the next time you encounter something that looks like a snake.

All too often in daily life our actions are based on incorrect perceptions or flow from destructive attitudes. We need to make a frequent reality check on our values and our viewpoints. The reality check of all life's situations is Jesus.

All of the Gospel narratives and sayings of Jesus are essential to a Christian view of life, but not all can be absorbed at one time. In each of the four books in this series we have concentrated on but one aspect of Jesus. In *Breaking Open the Gospel of Luke* we looked at Jesus' parables, in *Mark* at the humanity of Christ and in *John* at his divinity. In this book we concentrate on the attitudes of Jesus that give hope, peace and joy to life and lead to everlasting life. These are summarized in the Sermon on the Mount and are especially clear in the Eight Beatitudes (5:3-12) and in the Lord's Prayer (6:9-13).

How to Use This Book

This book does not cover every verse in the Gospel of Matthew. It focuses on the attitudes or the characteristics which Jesus said should identify the Christian. It focuses on the centerpiece of Matthew's Gospel, the Sermon on the Mount, exploring primarily the Beatitudes and the Lord's Prayer.

Nor is this book intended to be read at one sitting. It would be best to read and reflect on one section at a time. If you cannot immediately recall, at least in a general way, the story or sayings of Jesus referred to in the text, look them up in the Bible as you go along. The questions at the end of each chapter are intended to stimulate your thinking about the section and its application to your life.

Small-Group Discussions

The book is well suited for use by such small groups as faith-sharing communities, Bible study groups and spiritual reflection groups. The Gospels are intended to give life, not merely to be studied in an academic way. Hearing from other people about the impact a particular passage or saying of Jesus has had on a person's life or how others are struggling to be faithful to the gospel is often helpful and reassuring to the members of a group.

It is not necessary to finish a chapter at one setting. It *is* important to mull over the various ideas in the chapter. The text and questions are intended to spark sharing experiences and wrestling with the meaning of the Gospel among the members of the group. Not everyone in the group may see a connection between his or her own life and the attitude or characteristic under discussion. Yet, because most people will see some connection, it is important to keep the sharing on a personal level and not talk about "those people" out there or people in the news.

When a person talks about his or her own life or ideas, it is important to listen carefully and not interrupt, correct, lecture or give advice to the speaker. Everyone in the group should be given a chance to talk and no one should monopolize the conversation.

After a prayer (such as the one at the end of this Introduction), it is best to read a few pages aloud and then share the understanding, experiences or questions members of the group may have. The questions in the book are merely suggestions for starting a discussion on the ideas presented. Stop reading for discussion at any point when someone has a question or comment.

A leader or facilitator who has some biblical background could answer questions which come up in the group. If the group does not have a facilitator with this background, a commentary such as *The Jerome Biblical Commentary* or the *Study Edition of the Catholic Bible* may prove helpful with difficult passages.

FOR REFLECTION

Which of the Beatitudes below is easiest for you to practice? Which is the most difficult?

> Blessed are the poor in spirit, for theirs is the kingdom of heaven.
> Blessed are they who mourn, for they will be comforted.
> Blessed are the meek, for they will inherit the earth.
> Blessed are they who hunger and thirst for righteousness, for they will be filled.
> Blessed are the merciful, for they will receive mercy.
> Blessed are the pure in heart, for they will see God.

Blessed are the peacemakers, for they will be called children of God.
Blessed are those who are persecuted for righteousness' sake, for theirs is the kingdom of heaven. (5:3-10)

FOR PRAYER

At the beginning of each session pause for a short prayer for guidance and understanding—something like this:

Jesus, our model,
open our minds to grasp the meaning of your words,
our hearts to love them
and our wills to act on them. Amen.

Chapter One

In Search of the Author

S UPPOSE MATTHEW WERE on a book promotion tour and
we were having coffee with him after he had finished
signing copies of his Gospel. What questions might we
like to ask him?

It certainly would help us know Jesus better if we
knew something about Matthew's background, his reasons
for writing this Gospel and the sources of his information.
We also would want to know the main point of the book
and a few interesting facts about it. We would not expect
the author to go through it page by page, incident by
incident. We would hope that he could give us a clear
understanding of his core message in a few words. Of
course, we cannot sit face-to-face with Matthew and ask
our questions, nor do we have a record of such an
interview ever taking place. We can, however, look for
indications in his Gospel of how he might answer
questions such as these.

Unfortunately, the printed word gives us few if any
clues as to the identity and background of the author.
Nowhere is the author, the place of composition or the
intended audience mentioned. About the year 120 A.D., the
historian Eusebius identified the author as Matthew the
Apostle, but most scholars today do not agree with him.

They think that a person other than the apostle wrote it. We do not know who the actual author was.

This Gospel is based heavily on Mark. It seems unlikely that an eyewitness to the events would have followed another's account so closely. Mark wrote not long after the destruction of Jerusalem by the Romans in 70 A.D. It seems likely that Matthew wrote some years after that, perhaps around 80 A.D. Obviously, the author was a Christian who had a deep faith in Jesus Christ. The many direct and indirect references to the Hebrew Bible and to Jewish customs indicate that he was of Jewish ancestry and was writing for a community in which there were many Jewish Christians as well as Gentile converts.

Neither are there any indications as to where the Gospel was written. The best educated guess is that it was composed someplace in Syria, probably Antioch. Reading between the lines, we can discern that the author's community was going through a period of profound tension and change. Some members of the community had questions about Jesus, about his message and about how to lead the life of a disciple. Others were wondering why, if Jesus was actually the Messiah, the majority of Jews did not join them. Still other members were going back to Jewish observance.

There are also indications that there were external pressures on the community. Those who professed that Jesus was the Messiah and the Son of God had been excommunicated by the Jewish leaders. There had already been one serious Roman persecution. Added to these problems was the fact that a good number of Gentiles who did not know or observe the Law of Moses were coming into the Church, bringing with them different cultures and ways of thinking.

It seems clear enough that the community for whom Matthew's Gospel was written was struggling to find a new identity, a thoroughly Christian one. A careful study of the text shows that Matthew addresses all these issues indirectly in his accounts of the words and deeds of Jesus. Although some of the problems Matthew's community faced have been settled by time, we still can draw direction from what Matthew wrote in dealing with the questions we are facing today as individuals and as a community.

One question we most likely would like to ask Matthew in a personal interview would be why he wrote this Gospel when it seems that Mark had already written one. Nowhere does he give us an answer; we can only surmise his reasons.

The collection of sayings attributed to Jesus that were passed around were not enough to give a full picture of Jesus and of his teachings. Mark's Gospel had made a good start at recording the events of Jesus' life and his teachings, but it was sketchy in places. Reading between the lines, we can see that Matthew wanted to fill out some spots where Mark was too terse. Matthew wanted to record and pass on material that he possessed but which was not in Mark's Gospel. The people with personal experience of Jesus were dying off and their remembrances of the words and events in the life of Jesus were in danger of being lost.

Nor is it too difficult to see that Matthew was trying to reinforce the community's belief in Jesus and to settle questions people were asking about Jesus and the Christian life. Perhaps people wanted the words and deeds of Jesus in some organized form so that they would know what the apostles, most of whom were dead by the time, had preached. They also may have wanted this written record to pass their faith on to their children and to their children's children. But Matthew's reason for writing the Gospel is not as important to us as the reason we have for reading and accepting it.

FOR REFLECTION

Before we go on, it might be a good idea to stop and ask
ourselves quietly or discuss with the group:

1) *What two questions would I like the Gospel of*
   Matthew to answer for me about the teachings of
   Jesus?

2) *What two situations in the world today need to be*
   considered in the light of the Gospel?

FOR PRAYER

   Lord Jesus, our teacher,
   open our minds and hearts to your words and
     deeds
   as recorded in the Gospel of Matthew
   so that we may truly live in, with and for you.
   Amen.

Chapter Two

'The Kingdom of Heaven Has Come Near' (4:17)

ALTHOUGH WE CANNOT personally interview the author of the Gospel According to Matthew, we can do so in our imagination. In your mind's eye, see us transported back nearly two thousand years. We are in a large city in the Near East. People are coming and going. At the bookseller's shop the author has finished signing Matthew's name to the copies of the Gospel presented to him. We approach him and tell him we have traveled back through time. If he has time to speak to us, we would like to ask him some questions about his book.

He is astounded, but invites us to spend the rest of the afternoon with him. As we walk together through the street, he does not promise to answer directly the questions we have in mind. He does promise to guide us in our search for a deeper understanding of Jesus and his message.

We amble down to the house where he is staying. He offers us a comfortable chair and a cool drink. During our imaginary dialogue we will use the name *Matthew*, even though we are not sure what the author's real name is.

And we will intersperse our own reflections with his suggestions and answers.

Matthew nods and indicates that we can begin asking our questions. We pick up the scroll, point to the title and ask, "Why do you call your book 'Good News'? What relevance does it have for our lives two thousand years after you wrote it?"

Matthew's lengthy reply comes to something like this: "Think of this Gospel as a panoramic portrayal of the turning point in history. The frame in which that canvas is held is the promise that Jesus will be with us for all time. The angel announcing his birth called him Emmanuel, which means, 'God with us'—not for a mere few years, but always. The last words of Jesus on earth echo this promise, 'And remember, I am with you always, to the end of the age' (28:20).

"That is the Good News for you and for all people. Jesus came from the Father to be with his friends, not for a mere thirty-three years, but to be with them always."

We nod as he continues. "It is Good News for you so many years after my death because I have tried to help readers like you realize that Jesus is still alive and present among us. What I have written is not only an invitation to you to have a personal relationship with Jesus, but also an invitation to become a member of the community of believers, the Church.

"I tried to help people realize that those who believe in Jesus find that he makes a difference in their lives. He offers a way of life, a set of values, a complex of attitudes that present a goal worth pursuing and bring an inner peace that the world cannot give. His teachings and his life challenge the values that seem to offer these things but in reality are nothing but smoke. Jesus offers hope even when the situation seems to be hopeless. In times of change, uncertainty and transition such as we—and you—live in, Jesus is the light of the world shining in darkness, a solid rock on which to base one's life."

Our response to his words is an exclamation and another question, "That's a mouthful! Who is Jesus, do you believe?"

Matthew's reply is not an abstract set of propositions about the nature of Jesus. He suggests that we read his work and see that his answer is clearly stated in narrative form at the beginning, at the middle and again at the end of the book. These three sections will leave no doubt in our minds about Jesus' identity in Matthew's mind. Jesus is the Son of God, but he is also a human being who lived in the Middle East two thousand years ago. He is God become human.

At the beginning of his Gospel, Matthew explains that Jesus is a real human being and the rightful heir to the promises made by God to David, from whose line the Messiah was to come. He points to a long genealogy (1:1-17) to make this clear. We read and ask, "How does this genealogy tell us that Jesus is human?"

"First of all, it tells you who he is not. He is not like those nebulous pagan gods of ancient mythology who lived long ago in some unknown time and region. It tells you who his family was and the land and people in which he was born. He is a human being just like you. He was born at a specific time in history, as a member of particular people. The list also shows that he belonged to the House of David, from which the Messiah was expected to come. It shows that his ancestors were a mixed lot like most of yours: some good, some bad, some famous, others unknown. Jesus was fully human."

As we look more closely at the genealogy we see that there are gaps in the list, that the Hebrew Scriptures offer little or nothing about a number of the names on the list. And surely there were many more than fourteen generations between Abraham and Jesus! It is also interesting that women—Tamar, Rahab, Ruth and Mary—are accorded honorable mention, and that some of the ancestors of Christ (such as Ruth) were Gentiles. Nor were

13

all the ancestors of Jesus paragons of virtue. Jacob lied to obtain a precious blessing; Tamar was devious in her dealings with her husband and David was an adulterer.

The number fourteen is not to be taken literally. It is a multiple of seven, the perfect number in biblical thinking. Matthew explains that the perfect time had come for the Messiah and that details such as the exact number of ancestors are not important. He was not writing history as we know it. He is making a point about the humanity of Jesus. He is suggesting that his readers need to know something about God's actions in the history of Jesus' people and about their expectations of a savior or Messiah if they are to understand who Jesus is.

Secondly, Matthew makes it clear that he regards Jesus as God come among us in human form. In the story of the Annunciation (1:18-25), he tells of an angel announcing to Joseph that Jesus fulfills the prophecies and will be called Emmanuel, "God with us." In the middle of the Gospel he has Peter affirming, "You are the Messiah, the Son of the living God" (16:16). Finally, as Jesus hangs dead on the cross, Matthew puts a clear definition of his nature in the mouth of the soldier: "Truly, this man was God's Son!" (27:54).

As we read these passages we seem to hear Matthew turning the tables on us and asking us who *we* think Jesus is. In fact, he does pose that question to all the readers of his Gospel when he quotes Jesus asking his disciples, "Who do people say that the Son of Man is?" (16:13). Our answer does not lie so much in the words we use as it does in how we live. "Not everyone who says to me, 'Lord, Lord,' will enter the kingdom of heaven, but only the one who does the will of my Father in heaven" (7:21).

Doing the Will of God

Two small words in that injunction of Jesus catch our attention: *do* and *will*. We ask Matthew, "What is the 'will' of the Father and how do we go about 'doing' it?" The answer comes not in a sentence or two but in the twenty-eight chapters of the Gospel, beginning with the words, "The genealogy of Jesus the Messiah" (1:1) and ending with the words, "And remember, I am with you always, until the end of the age" (28:20). All the sermons, all the parables, all the sayings of Jesus as well as all the narratives about him tell us what the Father in Heaven wills us to do.

Before we ask more questions about the will of the Father and how we are to do it, we need to think about one word in the first verse of chapter three where Matthew pinpoints the first and most essential thing this "doing" involves. The one word is *repent*. It is sounded by John the Baptist as he marches out of his desert haunts to the banks of the Jordan river crying out, "Repent, for the kingdom of heaven has come near" (3:2). It is heard again when Jesus leaves the banks of the Jordan and sets up his headquarters in Capernaum, "Repent, for the kingdom of heaven has come near" (4:17). He was calling people to wake up, to become aware of a new way of being, to sense the presence and action of God in their lives.

The call to repentance is a call for a change of heart, a change of thinking, a change of values and attitudes. It is a challenge to see things in a new and different way. It revolves around the hope that something new will occur in us, that a door is opening, that life will make sense in this time of confusion and uncertainty. It is more than being sorry for this or that transgression and resolving to do differently in the future. It implies a complete change of heart and conduct, a new way of seeing self, God, neighbor and all of life. This change of heart is needed not only by those who are conscious of their sins and failings.

It is also required of those who are trying to keep the commandments but who also seek to have a "good" life. It is needed by those who have not completely assimilated the values of Jesus and made them their own.

Repenting demands that we become more aware of the way we view and interpret life. It calls us to notice in a new and different way what is going on in us and around us. We are incapable of taking in everything that is occurring in our lives. For example, experts tell us that thousands of impressions are bombarding our five senses at any one time, but that we are capable of being conscious of only five or six of them at one time. This limited capacity causes us to pay attention to certain things and ignore others. In a very real sense we pick and choose among all the data there before us. We think that what we see and the way we interpret what is happening in our lives is the correct and only accurate way to interpret it. To repent requires us to pay attention to things we once ignored and to ignore things to which we once paid close attention.

Repentance gives us a new focal point for our lives, a new vision of life firmly centered on the will of God. It gives birth to an attitude of hope and trust because we realize that God in Jesus is with us in even the most difficult situations. It causes us to become acutely conscious of the presence of God in our lives as well as in what is happening around us and to respond in love to that presence and activity.

The call to change one's way of seeing life comes not only to sinners who have neglected God and who have broken the commandments in very serious ways. It also comes to those who have tried to be faithful to the vision of life which Jesus offers.

The call comes in unexpected ways. Mother Teresa had been a faithful religious for many years and was doing a good job of teaching in a girls' school. Then one day she came across a man dying in the street with no one to care for him. Certainly she had encountered death before, but suddenly her usual way of seeing death and the poor was challenged and changed. With hope and trust she gave up the security she had as a teacher, left her community and founded a new order to care for the homeless sick and dying people of Calcutta as well as for abandoned babies. We say she had a conversion experience, but in truth she responded to a call to repent, to change her way of seeing the world. A new door opened for her.

Cardinal Joseph Bernardin of Chicago had a similar experience when he was told that he had a fatal cancer. He had been doing great work as a reconciler in the Church and as the administrator of a large archdiocese. It is hard to see that he had need of repentance, but he did see in the doctor's diagnosis a call to change his values, his view of life. In the last eighteen months of his life he spent as much time as he could in comforting other cancer patients.

What is meant by "a vision of life"? It is a frame of mind, a mentality, a way of interpreting reality often expressed in succinct words which carry a great deal of meaning to those who embrace them. For example, there is something we call the American way of life. This is not just two cars in every garage, three televisions in every home, a mobile phone and a modem for the Internet. More basically, it is a collection of ideas or ideals which guide the nation and the citizens. As individuals and as a nation we may not always live up to them, but we do profess them and try to implement them. We believe in *democracy*. In fact, we fought in two world wars to preserve this ideal for the world. We profess to protect the right of each individual to vote and to have his or her vote count. We believe in *justice and equality for all*. We impose sanctions on nations that do not respect human rights, and so on.

The call to repentance is a call to adopt the view of life Jesus had. The Gospels proclaim the ideas, the ideals, of that view of life and show that Jesus lived it in word and deed. Unlike him, even when we willingly, lovingly and joyfully embrace that view of life, we only partially succeed in living it out. We are people of our own times; our American culture often comes into conflict with the values of Jesus. At times it is rather easy for us to identify this conflict and to make a choice based on our faith, but at other times the conflict is not as apparent. Then we need to take time to reflect on our attitudes and motives and have the courage to change them and the direction we are going.

It seems obvious that Matthew's purpose in writing is to help us see what this new, this changed, vision of life is all about. It is to help us try to be persons like Christ, to develop the attitudes, ideals and values of Jesus. Matthew shows Jesus as having no doubts about how he would live his life. The joyful and stirring tune to which he dances in all situations is the will of the Father. Matthew indicates ways that tune was expanded and embellished, as well as the different tempos and keys in which it was played. The Gospel challenges those who wish to be disciples to learn this melody and the variations that interpret and reinforce it and to dance to them in the circumstances of their own lives.

FOR REFLECTION

1) *What is your reaction to the idea that some statements in the Bible, such as Matthew's genealogy, may not be historically accurate?*

2) *Recall a time when an unexpected event caused you to rethink the direction of your life. In what way did this involve repentance and a different way of thinking, feeling and acting?*

3) *Share an area in your life in which you hope something new will happen.*

4) *In what ways might being a Christian come into conflict with being a good American?*

FOR PRAYER

Jesus, you are the Christ who is always with us.
Help us identify the ideas, values and attitudes
that need to be changed or purified
if we are to follow you more closely. Amen.

Chapter Three

The Sermon on the Mount (5:1—7:28)

W E HAVE A DIFFICULT TIME understanding in what way we are called to change our values and our way of thinking. The ones we have seem to have served us pretty well so far. What more is required of us as followers of Jesus? We realize that the basic melody in Jesus' life was to do the will of his Father. We ask Matthew to tell us in a few words how Jesus sang that melody.

"Ah, yes," he replies, "A Pharisee once asked that question of Jesus in slightly different words when he wanted to know which was the greatest commandment. Jesus told him, 'You shall love the Lord your God with all your heart, with all your soul, and with all your mind.' This is the greatest and first commandment. And a second is like it: 'You shall love your neighbor as yourself'" (22:37-39).

"But," we retort, "love is such a nebulous attitude. It manifests itself in so many different ways in different individuals. We would like a more definite description of what we are to do in order to be loving people."

Matthew shakes his head at our lack of comprehension and directs us to the Sermon on the Mount, to the Beatitudes (5:3-12), which encapsulate the basic attitudes we need if we are to love God and neighbor. The other sayings in this sermon elaborate in practical ways how this melody plays out in particular situations.

Taking the hint from Matthew, we pick up his Gospel and read the first sentence of that Sermon. "When Jesus saw the crowds, he went up the mountain; and after he had sat down, his disciples came to him. He began to teach them saying..."

We stop right here and ask some questions, the answers to which may help us grasp more fully the importance of these injunctions for our own lives. "What is the significance of this sermon being given on a mountain? In Luke 6:22, Jesus delivers it on a stretch of level ground after he came down from the mountain, where he had been praying."

Obviously, Matthew wants to tell us something more than just the teachings of Jesus. In a subtle way he is stressing the authority of Jesus to say the things he did. In Scripture mountains are highly symbolic. They are where one meets God and hears the divine voice. For example, Moses, the great teacher of Israel, went up Mount Sinai, received the Ten Commandments, came down and delivered them to the people. Matthew sees one greater than Moses presenting a way of life that demands more than keeping the commandments. In fact, he has Jesus modifying the sacrosanct commands of Moses. Matthew does not present Jesus as a prophet thundering at the people, however. Nor does he present him as a king legislating the laws of the kingdom. He presents Jesus sitting down among his students or disciples, instructing them as a friend, sharing his view of life with those who are important to him.

Before we examine the text in detail we run our eyes over the subtitles in the three chapters which make up this sermon. (Of course, in Matthew's time there were no such things as chapters and verses. He wrote one continuous text, but we of the twentieth century arrange it into chapters, verses and subtitles.) The variety of subjects treated cause us to ask, "Did Jesus preach this sermon all at one time right at the beginning of his ministry?" The text seems to say he did, but because we find similar sayings being given in other places and at other times we can be certain that the entire sermon was not given at one time in one place.

First of all, the organization of the text makes it clear that Jesus did not one day lay down a list of laws similar to the Ten Commandments. Neither did he over the years carefully spell out a long series of do's and don'ts such as are found in the Pentateuch. Jesus moved around the country teaching in the synagogues and talking to individuals. People would present questions and cases to him and he would respond, stressing certain themes over and over again. Obviously, Jesus would have said the same things on different occasions and in slightly different ways. Later those who heard him would have remembered the punch lines of his talks or the answers to their questions. Perhaps some of these were even written down. Matthew pulled many of these together in one great sermon, the Sermon on the Mount.

In fact, to grasp the depth of meaning in each of the precepts in this sermon we need to reflect on each one in the light of the narrative sections of the book and in conjunction with the sayings uttered by Jesus at other times. The narratives often show Jesus himself practicing what he preached. His parables often illumine one or the other basic attitude embodied in the sayings recounted in this section. The precepts, the Beatitudes, the parables and the narratives express the same basic realities in different words.

There seem to be many hard sayings in this sermon. And so we ask, "For whom was this sermon intended?" For example, the Beatitudes have often been seen as applying primarily to the chosen, to those who aspire to a higher degree of spirituality. Those who do not have that kind of aspiration are expected merely to keep the commandments.

Perhaps this idea springs from the fact that Matthew seems to limit Jesus' words to his disciples, who came to him when he sat down to teach. But if we read through to the end of the sermon we find that Jesus was speaking not only to the group of disciples but to the crowds who came from all over the land to hear him. They were all "astounded at his teaching" (7:28).

Surely this sublime music was not meant merely for the few who walked with Jesus from place to place. It was meant for all those who come to him. It is the road map meant to guide whoever picks up Matthew's Gospel and accepts its message.

The Beatitudes

We turn back to the beginning of the sermon itself and quickly read over the Beatitudes. Each one begins with a promise of happiness, of joy and peace, of blessing. Each one challenges accepted ways of seeking happiness and peace. Each one frees us from self-interest and from self-pity. They seem to fly in the face of common sense. All our experience tells us that it is better to be rich than to be poor, to be happy rather than to mourn, to get even rather than to show mercy.

Our natural reaction to a first and superficial reading of the Beatitudes is to say that they are for the select few who are called to be contemplatives or those called to be saints. We instinctively want to sidestep their implications in our lives by saying that they are merely an ideal, a high ideal, but not practical in the real world of day-to-day struggles. We intuitively understand that the Beatitudes may call for drastic changes in our view of life, in our attitudes and in our behavior. We want to hang on to our way of thinking and acting, so we quickly slip into a defensive mode. We think of reasons why these admonitions will not work. We give instances that seem not to bring the rewards the Beatitudes promise. We know of people who are poor and not blessed or happy, of times when those who mourn have not been comforted, of cases where mercy has been misdirected. At a superficial reading we echo the King of Siam's comment about certain Western customs: "They are a puzzlement."

The Beatitudes differ from the Ten Commandments' specific do's and don'ts in that they are eight attitudes which can be expressed or violated in many different ways. They are based on faith and hope. Faith and hope are not necessary for observing the law; we *can* keep it out of fear of the consequences for breaking it. The law may produce a negative view of life, since it concentrates on the things we should not do. The Beatitudes depend on faith and hope because they call for a positive view not only of life's present confusion but also of the uncertain future. They tell us what kind of person we should be. A law person can too easily be caught up in the observance of externals. The Beatitude person is concerned about his or her internal attitudes. The law restricts our view of life to the thin line between sin and non-sin.

The law is like a hand-drawn map: If you miss a turn or depart from the route, you are lost. It does not aid you in seeing the beautiful and interesting places that lie off to the side of the road. The Beatitudes are like a giant topographical map that shows all kinds of interesting and beautiful things we can experience on the way. They call us to travel the byways and take new, unexplored paths.

We can also describe the Beatitudes as a powerful light that illumines our way. They reveal the beauty of living guided by God's vision rather than by our limited human sight. The eight of them are like a spectrum of the various wavelengths of light that coalesce into one bright white light to illumine God's will for us. They help us see the road to happiness as it really is, not as we think it is or ought to be.

We may well ask, "How do the Beatitudes throw light on Jesus' injunction to love God and neighbor?" The first four (5:3-6) primarily center on our relationship to God. The last four (5:7-11) primarily deal with our relationships with other people, and 5:11-12 amplifies the last blessing. These statements seem too simple. Yet they call for a great deal of reflection. Words spoken or even on a printed page can easily be misunderstood or interpreted in different ways. They can express ideas that seem cold and sterile, that stir little passion and enthusiasm in our hearts because we have had no profound experience of the reality they express. To make the Beatitudes an inspiring, motivating force in our lives we need to understand exactly what each of them means. We need to reflect on them in light of our own experience and the experience of others.

FOR REFLECTION

1) *The Reverend Dr. Martin Luther King, Jr., said, "I have been to the mountaintop"—referring to his vision of justice for all, black as well as white. When have you been to the "mountaintop" and seen a vision of a better way of life?*

2) *Recall and share a time when you saw someone put one of the Beatitudes into practice.*

3) *Which of the Beatitudes do you feel are most useful in today's world? Which are not very practical?*

FOR PRAYER

Spirit of God,
open our ears to hear the message of Jesus;
open our eyes to their application in our life
and open our hearts to receive and to share
   them. Amen.

Chapter Four

'Blessed Are the Poor in Spirit' (5:3)

T HE VERY FIRST BEATITUDE presents us with a problem: What is the meaning of "poor in spirit"? We look at Matthew and ask, "Who are the poor in spirit Jesus was speaking about? Luke speaks only of the poor (Luke 6:22). Are you talking about people who are down and out, discouraged, people with a broken spirit? Do you have in mind those who think poorly of themselves? Do you mean people who are humble? Or are you referring to people who are poor in material goods, people who are broke or living on the edge all the time? Or are you talking about people who have sufficient material goods but are detached from them?"

Matthew just smiles and asks, "What do you think?"

We realize that this is one of those sayings of Jesus which is best understood in the context of the subsequent understanding of believers. Certainly Saint Francis of Assisi, who owned nothing but the clothes on his back, was poor in spirit. But what of Saint Charles Borromeo, who used the great fortune at his disposal to help the poor?

The Hebrew Scriptures are full of references to the *anawim*, the poor who are the special concern of God. They were the people who put their trust entirely in God, not in themselves. They had no power and usually little money or security. They did not hold a position of influence in society or own many worldly possessions.

Matthew, in the narrative parts of his book, depicts people who were poor in spirit. One, at least, had some power and position: an official whose daughter had died. In spite of his position he realized that he had no one to turn to except Jesus, a man from God (9:18-19, 23-26). Others for whom Jesus worked a miracle most likely were actually poor in everything but trust. One was a woman who had been sick for many years with a hemorrhage (9:20-22). Another was a pagan woman, a Canaanite who asked Jesus to cure her daughter even after he had rebuked her (15:21-28). The poor in spirit are those who are humble and who place all their trust in the Lord.

George H. Gallup, Jr., cites some contemporary evidence that those who are materially poor more often tend to be poor in spirit than those who have some means and some power. He says in his book, *The Saints Among Us*, that his surveys tended to find the hidden saints mostly among people who are poor, less educated and non-white. His description of what he found could serve as a modern sociological description of the *anawim*.

> In many cases, these are people who have known dire economic straits, yet their faith has enabled them to step outside their grim conditions and find joy in life, so they run against the grain. The fact that they are downscale suggests that although they are burdened by economic problems, they are not overcome by them. They are more forgiving and more likely to be unprejudiced, as well as twice as likely to be involved in outreach to neighbors as people at the lower end of the spiritual commitment scale. In other studies we've done, such as on financial giving, we found that the poor give a larger proportion of their income to charity than the rich. Being surrounded by misery, they see opportunities to help on every side. The rich—especially now, with the widening gap between rich and poor—have a

tendency to cordon themselves off and therefore they
don't see much of the grimness of life.

Perhaps these people have grasped the core attitude
of the first Beatitude. They have had to put all their trust
in God because they realized from the circumstances of
their lives that they personally were powerless. However,
not everyone who is broke or having a hard time making
ends meet is poor in spirit. Such people can still be so
caught up in trying only by their own means to acquire
money and security that they do not put their trust in
God.

But it is not only the people living on the margin of
society who need this attitude. Although it may seem to
be easier for them than for people who are comfortably
well-off and who have some clout, every person is called
to this total reliance on God. Matthew makes this clear in a
narrative preceding the Sermon on the Mount. He relates
how a man who does have power, the power that is his as
Son of God, resisted the three basic temptations that
seduce people into thinking that they have the power and
the right to do what they would like to do rather than
doing the will of the Father. He tells us that Jesus went
into the desert to pray and there faced the tempter (4:1-10).
Questions as to whether or not Jesus fasted for forty days,
or was carried by the devil to a mountain from which he
could see all the kingdoms of the world, or even if the
tempter and the angels appeared in the flesh are incidental
to the message Matthew is presenting. They are details
that give graphic expression to the fact that Jesus made all
his choices based on the will of God, that he was a man
poor in spirit.

The three temptations are symbolic of all the
temptations to deviate from the will of God that mortals
have to face. They can be seen as temptations to the
pleasures of the body, to personal glory and honor or to
personal power. Yet basically they all are temptations to

pride, to doing things for one's own benefit in one's own way rather than according to the will of God. In this story we hear Matthew describing the fundamental struggle we all face.

Under the account of Jesus' struggle, Matthew seems to be telling us that life is not easy for any of us. In one way or another we will spend our forty days of fasting in the desert. Temptations to pride come our way in many forms. All sorts of people and situations challenge us to change stones into bread, to do something spectacular for the admiration of the mob, to fall down and worship the Evil One. This account of the temptations Jesus faced is a challenge to make our choices the way Jesus did—doing God's will and rejecting our inclination to personal ease, power and honor.

What are the attitudes of the poor in spirit that will color and guide all our decisions—not just the decisions about whether an action is sinful or not, but all the little daily decisions? Certainly there is the realization that all our trust must be in God because God is all and we are only what God has made us to be. A little later in the sermon Jesus expresses this basic attitude when he speaks about dependence on the God who clothes the flowers of the fields and feeds the birds of the air, while we cannot add one moment to our life span (6:25-34).

When some Pharisees tried to trip up Jesus by asking which is the greatest commandment, he touched on the basic attitude of this Beatitude: "You shall love the Lord, your God, with all your heart, and with all your soul, and with all your mind" (22:37). In other words, God must be first at all times in all situations.

It is easy to see how a statement such as this echoes the first Beatitude, but we ask, "Where do we find this single-minded attitude reflected in other sayings or events?" The text seems to murmur, "Read on." When we read the Parable of the Tenants who refused to pay their rightful due and killed the servants and even the son sent by the king (21:33-44), we see that these people were not acknowledging their dependence on the master. They were only thinking of what they wanted and of how they were going to take care of themselves.

The denunciations of some Pharisees and the woes pronounced on them flow from the fact that they were not poor in spirit but proud and self-centered, and that they did not practice humble, serving love (23:1-36). They made themselves number one instead of acting in a way that acknowledged their absolute dependence on God.

Jesus summed it up when he said, "All who exalt themselves will be humbled, and all who humble themselves will be exalted" (23:12). Leading up to this saying he cautions against calling anyone "rabbi," "father," "master" because we have but one teacher, one master, one father (23:8-10). At first glance this seems strange because we do have teachers and fathers and bosses or masters. Yet if we ask about the basic roles of these people we can see that they all impart knowledge, guidance and example, some of it sound and some of it not so sound. The only ultimate and only absolutely secure source of knowledge, guidance and example is the Father in heaven and his Messiah. That which comes from our teachers, fathers and masters on earth must always be viewed with the attitude of one who is poor in spirit and as such only totally trusts the knowledge, the guidance and the example of the Father and of his only Son.

Serving, generous, humble love is the basic attitude which guides all the actions of those who try to be poor in spirit. Jesus manifested this basic attitude of free, willing service when he cured a leper, healed the centurion's servant, restored Peter's mother-in-law to health, drove out demons, cured a paralytic, a blind man and a mute. We may try to excuse ourselves by saying that he was the Son of God and could do all these things, but that we are mere humans without that kind of power. That is true, but many, less spectacular human needs can be met by a person with a generous, humble, serving spirit.

At the end of his ministry Jesus returns to this theme once again. He gives us an indicator by which we can judge the depth of our commitment to God. Generosity in helping others rather than thinking of our comfort or pleasure is an indication that we are poor in spirit. Doing what the great King expects of us will usually require that we expend our material resources to help others. Jesus tells us that those who will possess the kingdom of heaven and see God feed the hungry, give drink to the thirsty, take in the stranger, clothe the naked and visit the sick and imprisoned (25:31-40). To help others in this way we need to have trust that God will take care of us. We need to be humble like little children (18:3).

The attitude which is contrary to that underlying the first Beatitude is self-centeredness. It is often expressed in phrases such as "me first," "doing my thing," "trusting in my own ability to do or be anything I want." This attitude takes credit for all the successes and good things in life and neglects to remember that God is behind them all. Digging into the Gospel and seeing the implications of the first Beatitude can be discouraging because we begin to realize how deep is our own self-centeredness, how high our opinion of our ability and gifts, how great our lack of appreciation for the gifts we do have.

In other words, we get a glimmer of the kind of false pride or self-centeredness that stands between us and possessing the kingdom of heaven. Matthew is sounding a call to wake up, to become conscious of what is going on within us and of what is going on around us. We all think we are conscious and awake, but are we? The first step in waking up is to begin to realize that the way we have seen life and made our decisions has not always been the best. We need to begin feeling uneasy, upset, discouraged, tired about the way we have been trying to run our lives and to acknowledge that, despite what we say, being poor in spirit is not our outstanding characteristic.

Our attitude toward the use of money can also make it difficult for us to be poor in spirit. Our society is based on consumerism. It judges the worth of people by how much they have and by their potential to get more. It stresses financial security and cannot understand the person who is not interested in making more money or the one who gives money away freely without considering whether or not the recipient is deserving. Saint Clement of Alexandria said in the third century that Christians were not to distinguish between the deserving and undeserving poor but, rather, to respond as if it were the Lord himself who was asking. He further says that Christianity is based on the unconditional and indiscriminate love of God who "makes his sun rise on the evil and on the good, and sends rain on the righteous and on the unrighteous" (Matthew 5:45). The generous giving of alms not only expresses our gratitude to God, it also deepens our dependence on the Lord and opens our eyes to the many gifts God has given us. Almsgiving, prayer and fasting are the foundation of a life of faith. They show that we are seeking to turn our lives over to God and to be poor in spirit.

FOR REFLECTION

1) *What does "poor in spirit" mean to you?*

2) *What is your reaction to the quote from George Gallup's book,* The Saints Among Us?

3) *What everyday temptations similar to those Jesus underwent make it difficult for us to be poor in spirit?*

4) *Which characteristics of being poor in spirit can you identify in the various miracles Jesus worked?*

5) *In what way do you find money posing a question about your trust in God?*

FOR PRAYER

My soul magnifies the Lord,
  and my spirit rejoices in God my Savior,
for he has looked with favor on the lowliness of
  his servant.
  Surely, from now on all generations will call
  me blessed;
for the Mighty One has done great things for me,
  and holy is his name.
His mercy is for those who fear him
  from generation to generation. (Luke 1:47-50)
Amen.

Chapter Five

'Blessed Are Those Who Mourn' (5:4)

T HE WORDS OF THE SECOND BEATITUDE there on the
page seem clear enough. But are they? Very few words
in the English language except scientific jargon have but
one clear and unequivocal meaning. Most words can mean
different things to different people. They have nuances
that we do not always take into consideration at the first
reading.

We understand words in the light of our own
experiences. Words bring back memories that color our
understanding of them even as we are trying to plumb
their meaning. For example, *to mourn* has a dictionary
definition, but our experience shades that meaning and
broadens or restricts its emotional impact. Mourning is a
sense of sorrow, a grieving because we have lost
something important in our life. Words that convey a
similar meaning are *grieving, sorrow, dejection. Brokenhearted*
is another way to put it.

Only our life experiences help us grasp the full
impact of that mourning. We mourn the loss of a pet, the
failure of a dream, the breakup of a relationship. We weep
because a painful cancer has caused a loss of health. We
are upset at losing our money when a pickpocket snatches
our wallet. We are brokenhearted because we have lost a

child, a spouse, a friend by death. In each case we feel grief or sorrow, but to a different degree and for a different length of time. It may be as short as a few minutes or it may last a lifetime.

As our interview with Matthew progresses we ask him, "What kind of mourning was Jesus talking about and what kind of comfort was he promising?" We would like Matthew to give us a clear, straightforward answer to our questions, but he does not. Instead he seems to ask us, "What have been your experiences of mourning? How have you felt? What has been your attitude toward the situations which cause you grief and sorrow? Have you put them out of your mind? Have you accepted them and made them part of your life? Have you learned anything from them? How have you been comforted and who has comforted you?"

The words of the text seem to say that the second Beatitude, as well as the other seven, will have little impact on our spiritual growth if we do not ask and answer questions such as these. The tremendous transforming power of the Beatitudes will not contribute much to the conversion of our attitudes and of our life unless our understanding of them has been intellectually deepened and emotionally colored by a personal experience. We cannot grasp the attitude toward life Jesus was talking about unless we know what it means both to mourn and to be comforted.

A priest tells a story that illustrated for him the human experience of mourning and being comforted more than words could.

> A parishioner asked me to visit her friend Margaret, who was dying of cancer. I had never met Margaret and was told that she was not a Catholic. Within minutes of my arrival at the cancer ward, she told me she was depressed and wanted to die. She asked in an abrupt manner, "Why won't they let me die?" She could see no reason for her suffering and felt

that God was far away.

On my second visit a few days later I sensed that there was a deep sorrow in her life and that she was angry and depressed. It turned out that her anger was directed at a daughter who was living in her house but who had not been to see her for quite some time. She was depressed because there was something she wanted to talk about with her daughter and was fearful that she would never see her again. After leaving the hospital I called the daughter and asked her to visit her mother.

When I visited Margaret the next day she was smiling, full of peace and waiting to see me. She told me that now she was ready to die because she and the daughter had "patched things up." She spoke of looking forward to seeing God face-to-face and that she knew that God loved her. She said that she had found such comfort in knowing that her daughter loved her and that she was now ready to "meet God."

She died the next morning. I never found out what went on between the two of them, but I had seen a person comforted who had been tormented by sorrow. I saw how love wiped away fear and healed wounds. I knew at a different level the kind of comfort Jesus promised to those who mourn.

An experience such as the priest had when he visited the dying woman throws great light on the second Beatitude. Love, forgiveness, reconciliation soothe the hurt of loss or of grief.

We ask, "What losses or sorrows will Jesus comfort?" This Beatitude does not promise to wipe out all pain and suffering. It does not promise that everything will be all right in this life if we but trust. A quick look at a crucifix shows that this is not true.

The mourning that will be comforted is being brokenhearted at losing God, at being at odds with God because of our sins. We mourn because we realize that as a result of our sins we may never see God. We mourn because we have failed to respond to the goodness and love God has shown us. We are sorrowful because we see on Calvary what our own sins as well as the sins of others have wrought on the God/man.

The comfort that will be given us is the assurance that God loves and forgives us no matter what we have done. The inner peace we experience when we recognize and accept this love brings comfort here in this life, but even greater comfort and love in the next life, in the Kingdom of God.

Any definition of *comfort* makes it sound cold. The experience of being comforted and images of those receiving comfort best convey the existential meaning of the word: a mother holding a sick child, a soldier cradling a dying buddy in his arms, an adult wiping tears from a child's eyes, a man with his arms around the shoulders of a friend who has just learned of his mother's death. The feelings associated with these images are hard to describe, but we know what they are: a sense of support, of understanding, of compassion, of love.

It does not take a lot of imagination to realize the joy and comfort the paralytic felt when Jesus saw him and said, "Courage, son, your sins are forgiven" (9:2). In fact, all the cures that Jesus wrought are signs to us that God does give comfort to people.

We take our mourning seriously in our hope that God does and will forgive us. Mourning for our sins and the sins of the world opens us to the tremendous reality of the freedom and forgiveness God gives us. We are forgiven even before we mourn, but we need to mourn so we appreciate the goodness and generosity of God. The comfort that comes to the one who mourns is inner assurance and peace that comes from knowing that things have been "patched up" with God even while we still live here on earth.

The comfort that will ultimately be ours is described in different words in the other seven Beatitudes. They all begin with the word *blessed*, which means "happy." This blessedness or comfort is described as possessing the kingdom of heaven, inheriting the earth, being filled, receiving mercy, seeing God and being called children of God. Those who live by the Beatitudes will enjoy the love and happiness that come from being in union with God.

Understanding the word *mourning* in its widest sense, we can see that we will grieve for more than our personal sins. We will feel the pain of all the evil in the world. We will also weep for the sins of the world. Jesus, who had no need to weep for his own sins, wept for the sins of Jerusalem and for those of all his people. Looking at the city with love, he lamented, "Jerusalem, Jerusalem, the city that kills the prophets and stones those who are sent to it! How often have I desired to gather your children together as a hen gathers her brood under her wings, but you were not willing!" (23:37).

Centuries before Jesus, the psalmist mourned not so much for his own sins as for the sins of the people: "My eyes shed streams of tears/ because your law is not kept" (Psalms 119:136). Any daily newspaper or TV newscast is enough to make a believer feel dejected, to be grieved at the condition of our society and of our world and to beg God to have mercy on this world.

When this sense of sorrow or grief motivates us to do something about these situations, God's comfort is experienced. A woman visiting Mother Teresa asked what she might do to help the abandoned babies. The aged nun picked up a crying baby and told her to comfort it.

There is yet another area about which the believer may mourn and be sorrowful. It is an area of life that cannot be traced to one person or even to one group of people. It is the structures and basic ideals, values and attitudes embraced by our society that are not in line with God's will for the human race. We recognize that many of the social, economic and political institutions in our country and in the world are cruel and unjust. As such they distance our society from God.

We weep for the collective selfishness which allows people to live in poverty in a land of plenty. We mourn that in so many areas of the world false nationalism causes young men to die in senseless warfare. We grieve because of institutional discrimination based on a person's race or religion. We shudder when we hear dishonesty justified as "good business practice." We mourn for society as a whole and for our participation in its sins.

This mourning is not the same as feeling sorry for the victims of injustice or feeling angry at the cause of human suffering. It is an awareness that collective sin attacks the dignity God has given each individual and very often keeps people from seeking and loving God as they are called to do.

Jesus encountered this kind of collective sin when he entered the Temple in Jerusalem and found people buying and selling there. It was the accepted practice. Everyone profited by it. The people bought what they needed for sacrifice. The sellers and priests made a living. What was wrong with it?

Jesus must have been angry because he overturned tables and chairs and said,

> It is written:
> "My house shall be called a house of prayer";
> but you are making it a den of robbers. (21:13)

His anger was a form of mourning and grieving at this disregard for God's house.

If we could actually interview Matthew in person, we might well ask him what we might do to absorb and appreciate the meaning this and the other Beatitudes have for our lives. He might give us a long talk about the meaning of each of the words or he might tell us more sayings and stories about Jesus. On the other hand, he might give us a bit of advice about how to do our own searching for the wealth in them. He might hold up a hand and say, "Slow down! Jesus did not rattle off these

Beatitudes all at one time. He gave them at different times in various situations. He gave his disciples time to think them over and slowly realize their meaning and implications.

"Take one Beatitude at a time. Chew on it! Go at it from different perspectives. Grapple with the various meanings and shades of meaning the words have if you wish to catch the full import of what Jesus said. Take your time! Your whole future depends on how well you assimilate these succinct guidelines of Jesus."

FOR REFLECTION

1) *Recall a time when you have had a small loss or a time when you have had a major, life-changing loss. What were your feelings and thoughts at the time?*

2) *How have others comforted you when you have mourned the fact that something precious has been taken from your life?*

3) *How does the Church bring comfort into your life through its sacraments and prayer life?*

4) *In what way do you feel a sense of mourning, grief or sorrow for the injustice and the sin you see in the world today?*

FOR PRAYER

Lord, we weep for what we have done and for what we have failed to do. Lord have mercy.
Lord, we weep for the sins of those who should know better but who have turned from you. Christ have mercy.
Lord, we weep for the social, economic and political sins of our country and of all the

countries in the world. Lord have mercy.
May almighty God have mercy on us, forgive
us our sins and bring us to life everlasting.
Amen.

Chapter Six

'Blessed Are the Meek' (5:5)

A QUESTION THAT RATTLES in the back of our minds as we sit facing Matthew during our imaginary interview with him is, "What sort of man is this who wrote such an extraordinary book?" From what we have read so far we can make a guess that he has a very positive and upbeat outlook on life. His is not the stern, joyless message some preachers pour into a microphone.

Right at the beginning of his Gospel he summarizes the teachings that Jesus must have repeated over and over again as he taught his friends the way to the Kingdom. Each of these eight insightful and powerful summary statements begins with the word *blessed*, that is, "happy." It is a strange list of things that make one blessed or happy, perhaps "at peace" would be better.

Placing the Beatitudes in such a predominant place in his manuscript indicates that Matthew must have realized their importance for the life of a disciple and must have tasted at least a bit of the happiness promised by Christ.

Of course, our next question is, "What does it mean to be happy? Is it that excited, warm fuzzy feeling we get when someone we love comes into the room or when we get a desired but unexpected gift? Is it to be without worries or to have all that we say we want?"

It is true that we often look for our happiness in some source outside ourselves, in some person or something we desire. But life's experiences teach us that no person or object, no position or bodily pleasure really makes us happy for a long time. Our relationships all have their ups and downs. At times they end. If we get a job we want, we get bored in time and begin looking for another one.

Happiness can only be found within ourselves. It comes from having a goal that gives meaning and direction to our lives. This goal only brings real blessedness and contentment when it reaches beyond this life to eternal life, to the good life in union with God. Matthew clearly saw this because he chose eight statements by Jesus that bring a good deal of interior peace in the present life but that will also bring complete happiness in a future life.

It sounds contradictory to say that being poor in spirit, mourning, being hungry and thirsty, suffering persecution bring peace of mind. Attitudes such as these are contrary to worldly wisdom and the natural desires of the human heart. Worldly wisdom tells us that good guys finish last, that if we do not look out for ourselves no one else will, that might makes right. Jesus turned this kind of thinking upside down.

"Blessed are the meek for they will inherit the earth" (5:5). Jesus' words echo those uttered by the psalmist centuries before, "But the meek shall inherit the land/and delight themselves in abundant prosperity" (Psalm 37:11). What is this land of which the meek shall take possession? The psalmist was talking about a piece of territory, the land of Israel. Jesus was talking about the true homeland of believers, the Kingdom of heaven, where they will find eternal peace, contentment, happiness.

Obviously, we need to ask, "Who are the meek who will inherit the land, who will win out in the long run?" It might be easier to describe who they are not. The meek of whom Jesus speaks are *not* the wishy-washy, spineless, submissive, subservient people we usually identify as meek. They are *not* people without backbone who have an indifferent, noninvolved attitude toward life. They *are* people who realize that they are not in complete control of their own lives and, especially, they are people who do not try to control the lives of others. Jesus respected the intelligence of others even when, as in the case of Judas, he knew what evil they were up to. He respected their freedom to make choices even if they had disastrous consequences.

Adjectives which describe the meek person of whom Jesus speaks are *mild, peaceful, unassuming, free from pride, enduring*. The meek are humble and gentle in their dealings with others because they realize their own littleness before the greatness of God. Machismo and a driving spirit of competition are not part of their makeup. A truly meek person is open and trusting, with a great deal of faith not only in God but also in other human beings.

Meekness is an acceptance that a particular aspect of reality is out of one's control; that one is not in charge but that all things are in the hands of God and one must rely on God's power and plan for life.

Such a meekness is often found in the early stages of 12-step recovery as a person recognizes that the problem or addiction is bigger than he or she can cope with, and it must be handed over to God who can deal with it.

The attitudes which characterize the meek person are practically the same as those of the person who is poor in spirit. Some scholars think that Matthew merely repeated the first Beatitude in slightly different words to emphasize its importance.

When Jesus invited those who were in need to come to him he did not mention his origin, his power, his destiny. He simply said, "Come to me, all you who are weary and are carrying heavy burdens, and I will give you rest. Take my yoke upon you, and learn from me, for I am gentle and humble in heart; and you will find rest for your souls.

For my yoke is easy, and my burden is light" (11:28-30).

Meekness and humility are not qualities that most people hold in high esteem. They are a way of life based on attitudes such as gentleness, self-control, total dependence on God and nonviolence.

On the other hand, control, independence, vengeance seem much more attractive. Yet Jesus said that we are to learn from him: The only way we can do that is to look beneath the surface of the things he did and identify the attitudes or virtues his action and words manifested. For example, if we put aside the miraculous nature of the cures in the eighth and ninth chapters of Matthew's Gospel, we can easily detect a meek heart that is gentle and sensitive to the sufferings of others. We see a caring heart that responds to people without looking for glory or its own aggrandizement. A man with leprosy approaches Jesus and professes his faith and trust. Jesus does something unthinkable. Before he heals the man, he touches him, breaking the taboo about contact with lepers (8:3).

A simple process of picturing the scene in the Gospel and asking what this incident tells us about being meek and humble of heart helps us uncover the nature of the meekness which characterized Jesus. As we read or listen to a narrative we hear not only the words but the tone of voice in which they were spoken. We ask, "Is that a false assurance that things will be all right in the long run or an invitation to trust in God?" We visualize the touch of Jesus and ask if it is a hearty slap on the back or a gentle contact.

We hear the frequent admonition to tell no one, and ask why Jesus would say something like that when one would think he would want the whole world to know about his power. Yet Jesus never advised anyone to go out and broadcast what he had done for them. There was nothing of self-aggrandizement in his miracles. Then we ask, "What does this attitude suggest to us about being meek and humble of heart?"

With Matthew watching us we examine in a

thoughtful way the miracles narrated by him in the eighth and ninth chapters. Take, for example, the cure of the centurion's servant (8:5-13). If you lived in an occupied country and a soldier humbly asked you for a favor, what would be your first reaction? As you picture Jesus in that situation, what do you read in his face as the centurion comes up to him? What tone of voice do you hear when he says, "I will come and cure him," when he praises the man's faith and tells him to go home because the servant has been cured (8:13)?

What runs across the screen of your imagination as you read the next simple but touching story (8:14-17)? Jesus and his friends have been traveling and preaching all day. They are hungry and tired. Peter invites them to his house for supper. As they enter the first thing they see is Peter's mother-in-law ill with fever. It looks as though there will be no meal this day.

Picture that scene: Jesus calling out for dinner, Peter making excuses for his mother-in-law, the sick woman embarrassed at being confined to bed when an important rabbi comes into her home. Meekness and gentleness are beautifully expressed in the words, "He touched her hand...and she got up...." Then in the evening, when Jesus should have been free to rest, he spends his time curing the other sick people in the village (8:14-16).

The meek man does not walk away from danger. If it is in his power to combat it, he does. Jesus was in a boat that was no bigger than a good-sized rowboat. A storm hit. The boat was in danger of being swamped. Fear of death seized the others. Some of that fear may have been in the pit of Jesus' stomach when he saw the height of the waves and felt the pitch of the tiny vessel. Yet he knew his own powers and he used them to help the others (8:23-27). Later Jesus asserted that he had the power to call the angels to his defense, but he did not do so (see 26:53).

Incidents such as these raise a question for us: When do we use the powers we have? And do we use them for our own advantage or only to help others?

It is extremely difficult to be meek when we are misjudged and falsely accused. Our usual response would be angrily to defend ourselves or to attack the person making the accusation. Our anger would show in our face if not in our words. Yet when the scribes accused Jesus of blaspheming after he told a paralytic that his sins were forgiven, all Jesus did was ask them a simple question and tell the man to "rise and walk" (see 9:1-8).

We read on about the cure of the official's daughter, of the woman with a hemorrhage, of the two blind men and of the man who was mute (9:18-34). After each story we stop, put ourselves into the scene and then ask ourselves a simple question: "What does Jesus say or do to show the attitudes that characterize a meek person?"

In fact, all of the miracles recounted in subsequent chapters give us a glimpse of a powerful yet meek man. The meekness of Jesus is most evident in Matthew 26 and 27.

In the Garden of Gethsemane Jesus expresses the fundamental attitude of the meek person in eight words as he addresses his Father in heaven, "Not what I want, but what you want" (26:39). When Jesus realizes and accepts the consequences of that will, we see a man at peace with his destiny, in control of himself and not fighting back at those who are set on his death. It is the picture of one who is waiting for God to act in response to his surrender to the divine will.

At first glance it would seem as though the meek are those who never act out of anger. Jesus spoke frequently against giving in to the impulse to anger. Moses had given the commandment, "Thou shall not kill," but Jesus went further and said that a person who is angry with another, who calls another an imbecile or fool will face judgment (see 5:21-22). Anger prompts us to retaliate. Mosaic law tried to keep retaliation at the level of the insult or injury, "an eye for an eye and a tooth for a tooth." The meek person does not retaliate at all, but turns the other cheek (see 5:38). To this admonition Jesus added the most difficult command for those who have anger in their hearts, "Love your enemies and pray for those who persecute you" (see 5:43-47).

Yet this appraisal that anger has no place in the heart of the meek person is not wholly correct. The meek do not react in anger to insult or injury directed at themselves, but often they react with righteous anger at injuries or injustices directed at others or at God.

Their reaction, however, is not violent. They try not to escalate the cycle of violence by being as violent or even more violent than an oppressor. Any form of resistance to evil requires courage, but it takes more courage to resist evil by nonviolent means than by violent ones. In our own century we have seen how the domination of a colonial power, Britain, was overthrown by the nonviolent revolt of Mahatma Gandhi and how the bars of segregation were torn off one by one with the nonviolent resistance the Reverend Dr. Martin Luther King, Jr., preached.

Meekness and an understanding heart give birth to forgiveness. It is visible when a mother forgives the murderer of her child, and its opposite is evident when we see a mother cursing such a person.

A soft word, a meek word, is a form of nonviolence. It has tremendous power to calm a volatile situation in the home. Speaking softly and slowly will often calm a screaming child or defuse an angry exchange of words. On the other hand, sometimes the meek person has to be firm and to take action. Jesus was not the picture of meekness when he overturned "the tables of the money changers and the seats of those who sold doves" in the outermost court of the Temple area (21:12, 13).

Aristotle saw meekness as the happy medium between too much anger and too little. People with too little anger are lethargic, indifferent to injustice, insensitive to suffering and really out of contact with what is going on around them. People who impulsively act out of anger often strike out when there is no reason to strike out, doing more harm than good. Meek persons have self-control, but recognize their own weakness and so put themselves under the complete control of God.

In *The Gospel of Matthew*, Scripture commentator William Barclay writes that the Greek word for *meek* had three meanings: control of anger, self-control and true humility. He offers an expanded version of the third Beatitude that encompasses all these meanings:

> O the bliss of the man who is always angry at the right time and never angry at the wrong time, who has every instinct, and impulse and passion under control because he himself is God-controlled, who has the humility to realize his own ignorance and his own weakness, for such a man is a king among men!

FOR REFLECTION

1) How would you define meekness?

2) Being meek means to accept reality without being angry or bitter. Recall someone you know who, in the face of great difficulties, was able to accept the situation peacefully as God's will. What was the situation? What was the outcome?

3) Recall a time when you were hurt by some situation but you responded with openness and patience. What emotions and or temptations did you need to let go of? What was the outcome?

FOR PRAYER

God, give me the serenity
to accept the things I cannot change,
courage to change the things I can,
and the wisdom to know the difference.

Chapter Seven

'Blessed Are Those Who Hunger and Thirst for Righteousness' (5:6)

O UR INTERVIEW WITH MATTHEW moves along, but the afternoon is growing warm. Matthew asks whether we might like a drink and perhaps a sweet to go along with it. We take up his offer for a cool drink, but pass on the sweets.

Food and drink are a universal sign of hospitality because they are so vital for life. The need for them is never far from our consciousness. Hunger and thirst are powerful metaphors for a strong desire. In Matthew's time they carried even more impact than today. We in the modern Western world fear drought and famine not as threats to our lives but only as strains on our pocketbooks. If there is a crop failure in central California, we bring in more vegetables from Mexico. We use tanker trucks if the water system fails.

When we say we are hungry, we usually mean that it is mealtime or that we want a snack. When we say we are thirsty, we usually mean we want to go to the water cooler or to the fridge for a cola. The only contact most of us have with the kind of hunger or thirst that causes people to die is through pictures of people starving in Africa, India or China.

In Matthew's time hunger and thirst were more powerful motivators than they are now. If there was a natural disaster and crops failed, people starved to death. If the rains did not come for several years, the wells and cisterns ran dry and people died of thirst. Most of the people at some time or other had to devote all their thought and energy to finding food or water. Hunger and thirst were the driving force in their lives.

When Jesus said, "Blessed are those who hunger and thirst for righteousness," he was making the search for righteousness the number one priority in a person's life. It is to be the driving force that supersedes all other goals, ambitions and desires. He said the same thing in other words a bit later in the Sermon on the Mount when he told those who were concerned about what they should eat or drink or wear to "strive first for the kingdom of God and his righteousness, and all these things will be given you as well" (6:33).

The hunger and thirst of the soul is different from that of the body. When we are physically hungry or thirsty, we are satisfied when we have something to eat or to drink. The need slips out of our consciousness until it arises again some hours later. The hunger and thirst for righteousness that Jesus promises to satisfy is different. The more we experience the goodness of God in our lives, the greater is our desire for more. Our spiritual hunger and thirst is never satisfied while we walk on this earth.

"Ah, yes," we say. "We must desire with our whole heart and soul to find God, to be united with God, to enter the kingdom that begins here on earth and continues eternally in the next life. But what must we *do* to achieve this goal? We have to work hard to earn our physical food and drink. What kind of things must we do to have our hunger for union with God satisfied?"

The answer to this question is a paradox. One part of the answer is, "Nothing except to want it." We can hunger and thirst for it, but nothing we do can make us deserving of this gift. We need, however, to cooperate with God and freely respond to God in order to receive God's gifts. Thus, the other part of the paradox is that we should try our best to live by the commandments and the ideals of Jesus. What is the use of trying to live in conformity to the will of God if we cannot earn a reward for following it? This is where the paradox lies. God is good; God's heart never closes to people's feeble efforts to please him. The Psalmist says,

> The LORD knows the days of the blameless,
>   and their heritage will abide forever;
> they are not put to shame in evil times,
>   in the days of famine they have abundance.
> (Psalm 37:18-19)

The efforts we make to live by the words of Jesus, and especially the attitudes from which they flow, dispose our hearts to accept God's offer of friendship. Trying as best we can to live according to the commandments and to follow the words of Jesus is a way of thanking God ahead of time for the gift of righteousness or holiness when it is offered to us.

What is this righteousness we are to seek so avidly? The Greek word for *righteousness* is translated in various ways. Each gives this Beatitude a different direction. The Jerusalem Bible translates it as "Blessed are those who seek what is right." Other translations use the word *justice*, implying that the people who seek to bring justice to the poor and needy will be satisfied. Long experience shows that this is not necessarily so. In fact, those who seek justice in this world seldom have their fill. They fail more often than they succeed.

A better understanding of the word *righteousness* would be that it means the holiness of God, the saving activity of God. Thus the direction of the Beatitude would not be toward something to do, but rather toward openness to a gift we desire most vehemently, namely the saving grace of God. The righteousness that will satisfy the hunger and thirst of the human heart is the kingdom of heaven, union with God.

This personal union with God is inseparable from the love of our neighbor, however. In the Old Testament doing justice summed up the commandments because acting justly toward one's neighbor was essential for keeping the covenant. A just person was one who acted like God: showing compassion to those in need, righting the wrongs done to them and rescuing them from harm. This call to act justly was modeled by God, who heard the people's cries in Egypt and came to their rescue in the Exodus event. Later prophets condemned ritual worship that is not connected with justice and they targeted widows, orphans and aliens as special recipients of one's concern (Isaiah 1:11-17; 58:1-11). Jeremiah cried out that to practice justice is to know God (Jeremiah 22:13-16).

In the New Testament love of God, neighbor and self is the summation of Jesus' teaching. For Jesus, love comes from the heart of the person and has its foundation in the love of God. To hunger and thirst for union with God is to express compassionate love toward those in need. It is a movement of the heart that feels the pain of another and impels us to act with loving generosity. Our love of God is both motivation and empowerment to reach out to others. Jesus was constantly moved by compassion as he healed, fed the crowd and taught those hungry for the words of life.

To hunger and thirst for righteousness is to be moved to action. We can think of many people who, motivated by a desire to love God, have undertaken new and courageous action on behalf of others. Great saints like Francis of Assisi, Vincent de Paul and Mother Seton were moved by compassionate love to help others in need. In our own day Cesar Chavez and Dorothy Day strove to better the lives of people by helping them and by working to change the structures that held them bound.

Saint Augustine expressed the core of this Beatitude when he said, "O God, our hearts are restless until they rest in thee." Awakening all around us are signs of this restlessness, this hunger and thirst. They are obvious in the effort and time people put into the various renewal programs of the Church. They are evident in the number of people who are seeking personal spiritual direction. But they are also evident in people who are seeking a deeper spiritual life outside the mainstream. Programs abound that promise to help people learn how to find inner peace and to deal with various addictions and other stresses of daily life. Signs of this hunger are evident in people seeking peace and tranquility and a deeper meaning to life through Eastern meditation, Native American practices or even ancient pagan rites. They are looking for something that will give them a clear, positive and ultimate purpose in life. They are looking for God, for the Kingdom.

Most of these efforts make it clear that fulfillment does not come from things outside ourselves but from something inside, from knowing ourselves, from overcoming negative influences, from becoming detached. Most hold that individuals can find truth, ultimate goodness and meaning within themselves. In this they are highly individualistic and suspicious of organized religion. Most proclaim that they are spiritual but not religious; they associate religion with authority that they consider oppressive and with doctrines they feel they cannot believe.

The desire for spiritual growth is not to be ridiculed wherever it appears. All these efforts suggest something about how one opens oneself to the activity of God. Surely more people need to meditate. Surely, more people need to eschew the rat race. Surely, more people need to take time to smell the flowers and be in tune with nature.

But once our hearts have begun to hunger for God we feel need for the Church, for organized religion. Organized religion gives us norms for discerning the value of what we find when we go into ourselves. In human nature there is much that is good, but there is also a tremendous tendency to selfishness and other forms of evil. We need to know how to judge that we are not merely canonizing our own desires and are truly in touch with the Spirit.

Even when we encounter the Spirit, we need norms that keep us from trying to make a house pet out of the Spirit instead of allowing that powerful whirlwind to lead us where it wills. The Spirit of God is not always a gentle breeze. More often than not it takes us in directions that we might not ordinarily choose to go.

Further, the Church has handed on the experiences and wisdom of people who have made the journey before us. This knowledge helps us avoid reinventing the wheel, learning the hard way once again. Trappist monk Thomas Merton discovered that, after going around the world investigating various other traditions of meditation, there was nothing he could be taught that he could not have found already existing in his own monastic tradition.

Finally, the Church constantly keeps before us the fullness of the meaning of this Beatitude. Union with God is not an end in itself. It cannot be separated from a loving, caring union with our neighbors. When we are tempted to concentrate on our own growth and peace, the Church forcibly calls us to affirm the dignity of all human beings in all circumstances of their lives. Through its living tradition the Church identifies for us many issues and conditions that demand a response in faith. It reminds us that a genuine hunger and thirst for justice reaches out to all areas of life. It needs to be expressed concretely not only in prayer and contemplation but also in loving service to those who suffer from economic and social injustice, from war and famine, from corrupt political systems and from illness. The Church helps us see that, if we say we love God, we must be concerned with protecting and using the bounty of God's creation for the benefit of all.

A view of life this broad makes us single-minded. This attitude is like the eye that is the light of the body and that, when sound, gives light or direction to the entire body (6:22-23). This single-mindedness causes a person to sell everything in order to buy the field in which the treasure is buried or the pearl of great value (13:44-46).

Each of the Beatitudes needs to be seen in relationship to one another. As was mentioned earlier, there are various ways to categorize them. We have chosen to see the first four as relating primarily to the attitudes we have as we face God and the last four as relating primarily to our attitudes in dealing with our fellow human beings.

The attitudes expressed in the first three are all in some way necessary if we are truly to hunger and thirst for the fulfillment that can be found only in God. They are steps in the process of opening ourselves to God and receiving God into our hearts. Being poor in spirit is the realization that we are dependent, that we are not totally in charge of our lives. Mourning or repentance follows this realization because we recognize how often and badly we have failed in our efforts to love God and neighbor. Being meek involves self-surrender to God because we know that we cannot change by our own power. We have to put our lives in the hands of God. These three attitudes stir up a hunger and thirst in us for fulfillment, for salvation, for redemption, for the Kingdom that God freely gives.

FOR REFLECTION

1) *In your own words, how would you express the role of good works and of faith in your journey to heaven?*

2) *Describe an injustice about which you feel passionate. What have you done about it?*

3) *What would you say to a person who says that he or she is spiritual but not religious?*

FOR PRAYER

As a deer longs for flowing streams,
  so my soul longs for you, O God.
My soul thirsts for God,
  for the living God. (Psalm 42:1-2)

O God, you are my God, I seek you,
  my soul thirsts for you;
my flesh faints for you,
  as in a dry and weary land where there is no
  water.
So I have looked upon you in the sanctuary,
  beholding your power and glory.
Because your steadfast love is better than life,
  my lips will praise you. (Psalm 63:1-3)

Chapter Eight

'Blessed Are the Merciful' (5:7)

B Y THIS TIME our imaginary interview with Matthew has been going on for some time. We take a long break for dinner and come back to the interview in the relaxed cool of the evening. As we settle down in our chairs we realize that Matthew has been asking us as many questions as we have been asking him. This thought makes us bold enough to resume our conversation with a comment rather than a question: "The first four Beatitudes offer a great deal of hope, but do not seem to spell out in any great detail what we need to do. They seem to reflect the passive attitude of a person who is waiting to be given something. They seem to imply that if we have the right dispositions we can sit back and wait for God to give us the land, to comfort us in our worries and to satisfy our desire for holiness, truly to bless us."

We look at Matthew and ask, "Are we expected to do anything to enjoy this blessing? If so, what are we to do?" Matthew's eyes open wide at this question. They seem to say, "Don't you understand that the attitudes those first four Beatitudes express will motivate a person to act in the right way?" But instead of saying anything he taps the next four Beatitudes with his finger, points at the rest of the Sermon on the Mount, indicates a large section on the miracles of Jesus (chapters eight and nine) and with a flourish places his finger on a later passage:

> Then the king will say to those at his right hand, "Come, you that are blessed by my Father, inherit the kingdom prepared for you from the foundation of the world; for I was hungry and you gave me food, I was thirsty and you gave me something to drink, I was a stranger and you welcomed me, I was naked and you gave me clothing, I was sick and you took care of me, I was in prison and you visited me.... [J]ust as you did it for one of the least of these who are members of my family, you did it to me." (25:34-35, 40)

The gesture of running his finger down through the scroll conveys to us more clearly than words that no text or even group of texts can be taken in isolation. Each text needs to be understood in relation to what has been written before and after. They are part of one message. We can appreciate the power and importance of the first four Beatitudes for our lives only when we reflect on them in the light of the last four and in conjunction with the narratives and sayings of Jesus recorded in the rest of the Gospel. A truly Christian outlook on life depends on our ability to see the message as a whole, each section casting light on the other sections. It depends on our ability to look at particular sections, stand back from them and see in the light of the whole what is basic in them. Then we will more clearly know what is required of us.

With this clearer understanding of the best way to get to the heart of an individual Beatitude, we ask Matthew, "What is mercy? What other texts in this Gospel will throw light on this Beatitude?"

As is his habit, Matthew throws the first question back at us. We realize that each of us has some idea of the meaning of mercy. We realize also that our understanding of that word as it applies to our own lives is colored by our experiences of receiving and giving mercy.

We reach for the *Oxford English Dictionary*, which defines mercy as "forbearance and compassion shown by one person to another who is in his power and who has no claim to receive kindness." This definition implies forgiveness even though the other person rightly deserves punishment. Mercy reaches out in forgiveness to soothe pain and heal wounds. In popular usage, to show mercy also means to help a person who is in some kind of need, especially if that person has no claim on us.

What other passages in Matthew's Gospel help us comprehend what Jesus meant when he spoke about mercy? We have but to look at the second Beatitude, "Blessed are those who mourn, for they shall be comforted," to identify the basic attitude that is the source of merciful actions. The mourning of which Jesus spoke is the humble, dependent, repentant attitude that comes from the realization that we are sinful, broken human beings, in need of God's compassion and forgiveness, in need of God's mercy. This attitude, together with the realization that God has extended mercy to us and has already comforted us, motivates us to be grateful and to show that gratitude by being merciful to others. In other words, the mourning of which Jesus spoke is most genuine when it mirrors to others the comfort, the forgiveness, we ourselves have received.

Bill Wilson, cofounder of Alcoholics Anonymous, experienced the mercy and compassion of God through the concern of a friend who had been an alcoholic like himself. The friend, now sober, wanted to share his recovery journey with Bill. He declared that God had done for him what he could not do for himself. His human will had failed. He could not stop drinking. He recognized that by himself he was powerless to stop drinking. With that insight he realized that he had to make a complete surrender of his life to God, the higher power. This he did. Now he was offering this experience as a possible road for Bill to follow.

Wilson accepted the challenge and surrendered his life and his alcohol addiction to God. Later he declared:

> It melted the icy intellectual mountain in whose shadow I had lived and shivered for many years. I stood in the sunlight at last.... There I humbly offered myself to God, as I then understood Him, to do with me as He would. I placed myself unreservedly under His care and direction. I admitted for the first time that of myself I was nothing; that without Him I was lost. I ruthlessly faced my sins and became willing to have my new-found Friend take them away, root and branch. I have not had a drink since. (*Alcoholics Anonymous*, Alcoholics Anonymous Publications, 1955, pp. 12-13)

Bill Wilson experienced what it meant to be poor in spirit. He was powerless, but he did not realize that God could and would supply the power he needed to stop drinking. His friend extended to Bill the mercy, compassion and power of God which the friend himself had experienced. Bill and his friend then proceeded with a small group of friends to extend that mercy and compassion to others seeking to find their way out of addiction to alcohol. They developed the famous "Twelve Steps of Recovery" that are the basis of Alcoholics Anonymous and many other recovery programs.

The fifth Beatitude promises that the one who is merciful will receive mercy. This reward will be given not only at the Last Judgment and in a future life, but it will also come to us here and now. It came to Bill Wilson when, as he said, he came into the sunlight out of the shadow of the icy mountain. We are blessed because mercy frees us from carrying around the burden of the hurts and injuries that we feel have been inflicted upon us. It brushes them aside so that they do not color our thinking and actions. It sets us free to see life and make decisions independent of the control of resentments, anger, hurt feelings and the desire for revenge. It also frees us from attempting to control or manipulate another to do our will or from trying to diminish them by showing our superiority in knowing what is right and just. With this freedom comes inner peace, a blessing indeed.

Jesus frequently made the connection between the forgiveness and mercy we receive and the forgiveness and mercy we are expected to extend to others. When he told his disciples how to pray he said one of the petitions should be, "Forgive us our debts, as we also have forgiven our debtors" (6:12). He promised them, "For if you forgive others their trespasses, your heavenly Father will also forgive you" and added a warning, "but if you do not forgive others, neither will your Father forgive your trespasses" (6:14-15).

In his sermon about the last judgment Jesus graphically described the reward to be given on that day to those who show mercy and compassion as well as the punishment intended for those who do not. The reward is that which is promised in so many different ways by the Beatitudes: eternal life and the peace that comes from being in a reciprocal loving union with God. The punishment is eternal.

> "Come, you that are blessed by my Father, inherit the kingdom prepared for you from the foundation of the world; for I was hungry and you gave me food, I was thirsty and you gave me drink. I was a stranger and you welcomed me, naked and you gave me clothing, I was sick and you took care of me, I was in prison and you visited me...." Then he will say to those at his left hand, "You that are accursed, depart from me into the eternal fire prepared for the devil and his angels; for I was hungry and you gave me no food, I was thirsty and you gave me nothing to drink, I was a stranger and you did not welcome me, naked and you did not give me clothing, sick and in prison and you did not visit me." (25:34b-36, 41-43)

Offhand, these words of Jesus seem to make the

mercy God extends to us depend on our first being merciful to others. They seem to put a condition on the unlimited and undeserved love God extends to all people. It is true that God is good and loving and freely extends forgiveness for anything we do even before we ask for it. But that forgiveness needs to be acknowledged and accepted by a heart which shows itself grateful by being merciful to others. It is not that God refuses to forgive or makes that forgiveness dependent on some action of ours. Rather, our heart that refuses to forgive and to show compassion to those in need cannot be penetrated by God's mercy and so it is wasted on us. Our hard and unfeeling hearts condemn us to eternal punishment in the loveless lair of the devil and his angels.

Many of the other sayings of Jesus in the Sermon on the Mount relate in some way to mercy. Matthew quotes Jesus as saying, "Be perfect, therefore, as your heavenly Father is perfect" (5:48), while Luke cautions, "Be merciful, just as your Father is merciful" (Luke 6:36). We are never more like our God than when we forgive freely and from the bottom of our heart.

If we ask how are we to live out other sayings of Jesus, being merciful is one of the most obvious answers. For example, if we ask, "How are we to be the salt of the earth and the light of the world by which the heavenly Father is glorified?" (see Matthew 5:13-16), the answer is by extending the mercy of God to others. If we inquire, "What is it that cools the fires of anger that cause us to insult and even kill a brother?" (see 5:21-22), mercy immediately pops into mind. If we examine what it is that motivates us to love our enemies, to turn our cheek when someone strikes us, to go the extra mile with the one who imposes on us (5:39-47), we see that only a humble and merciful heart can motivate us to question the human wisdom that justifies revenge in these situations. If we probe our reasons for passing judgment on people (7:1-5) and seek to refrain from that arrogant behavior, we need to acknowledge our own faults and our own need for compassion and understanding. Finally, it is impossible to live by the command, "In everything do to others as you would have them do to you" (7:12), without extending to others the understanding, mercy and forgiveness we want for ourselves.

But it is not only the sayings of Jesus that suggest ways in which we can show mercy to others. In chapters seven, eight and nine Matthew recounts many of Jesus' miracles. From these we can gather some basic norms to guide us in our efforts to show mercy to those in need. Jesus extended his help to those in need whether or not they asked for his help. He laid down no conditions and asked no questions about the worthiness of the person. The leper cries, "Lord, if you choose, you can make me clean," and is healed (8:1-4). Peter's mother-in-law was laid low with a fever; Jesus touched her and she was cured (8:14). No fuss was made about any of these cures.

Matthew also puts his finger on a very important element of mercy: pity. He concludes the long list of miracles by saying that Jesus' heart was moved with pity at the sight of the crowds because they were troubled and abandoned (9:38). He cured their illnesses and diseases and gave them hope with his message.

Jesus' parables, especially those pertaining to the Kingdom, are also closely related to the Beatitudes, especially to the fifth one. The connection is clear in the story of the unforgiving servant who had a tremendous debt remitted by his employer, but who demanded the last penny owed him by his fellow servant (18:23-35). There is no place in the Kingdom for an unforgiving heart. Who is the man who comes to the wedding feast without wearing a wedding garment (22:2-14) but the person whose heart is not clothed in mercy? There are many ways to understand the parable of the talents (25:14-30), but it does not take a great deal of effort to see the talents entrusted by the master to his servants as the mercy God entrusts to us. If we accept it and hug it to our heart, are we not burying it instead of multiplying it in the world?

This Beatitude throws light on the parable of the wheat and the weeds that grow together in a field (13:24-30). Who are the wheat but those who grow in mercy and love? Who are the weeds but those who do not forgive or show mercy? The same is true of the net cast into the sea which brings ashore the haul to have the good and the bad separated (13:47-50). With a little reflection practically all of the narratives and sermons of Jesus will reveal facets of mercy because the God Jesus revealed is the God of mercy.

The Scripture narratives are so familiar that often their impact is blunted. The sayings of Jesus are repeated so often that they sound like mere cliches. Two photos that appeared in the news in recent years capture better than words the essence of mercy. One published several years ago showed Pope John Paul II in a Roman jail, offering forgiveness to the man who tried to assassinate him in St. Peter's Square. The other, more recent, showed Cardinal Bernardin visiting and forgiving a young man dying of AIDS who falsely accused him of sexual misconduct years earlier. These two pictures illustrate the fifth Beatitude in action.

Pictures such as these also raise questions for us, questions which are not easily answered. For example, how do we reconcile compassion with justice? What are the offenses that I feel I cannot forgive under any circumstances? Who are the people I refuse to forgive and why?

Neither Jesus nor Matthew gives us answers to questions such as these. Besides the objections that our anger, pride and our sense of justice raise against mercy in particular cases, we have to struggle with the negative attitudes in our culture. Our society on one hand justifies euthanasia and assisted suicide in the name of mercy. On the other hand, it calls for extending the death penalty to more crimes and votes to tighten welfare benefits without adequate protection for people who are psychologically unable to care for themselves.

Struggling with these questions, we ask, "What can I do to learn to be more merciful and forgiving?" Again there is no simple answer, but there are a few things we can do which might help us become more worthy of the blessing promised to the merciful.

1) One kind deed, one act of forgiveness does not make a heart merciful and generous. Such a heart is formed by the day-to-day effort to look kindly on those who have hurt us in word or deed. It is shaped by recognizing our own faults and brokenness, our frequent need for mercy and forgiveness. It is structured by understanding the reasons people may have had for treating us as they did and the reasons we have for treating them as we do. It is molded by our efforts to learn to live with the faults of imperfect human nature—our own as well as those of others.

2) Reflecting frequently and prayerfully on the life and teaching of Jesus will enlighten our intellect and help us realize how much we need forgiveness from God and the dire results of not being merciful to our fellow human beings.

3) Recognizing honestly what is going on within us when we feel anger or the impulse for revenge and acknowledging that the problem is ours, not the other party's, is a giant step forward in nourishing a merciful heart. We cannot change other people. We are not in charge of their lives. But we can change ourselves and the way we look at situations. We can make mercy a higher priority than justice. Grasping this fact, we can lay out a plan of action that seeks peace and reconciliation instead of revenge.

Being merciful is difficult. It seems to go against human nature, but the reward is worth the struggle: "Come, you that are blessed by my Father, inherit the kingdom prepared for you from the foundation of the world" (25:34).

FOR REFLECTION

1) How would you define mercy?

2) Jesus asks us to recognize the brokenness in our own lives and then to use that as a way of seeing the pain in the lives of others. Recall an event in your life that helped you be merciful and compassionate to someone who was in a similar or identical situation.

3) What is the most vivid picture you have in your memory of someone who is compassionate and merciful?

4) What other trends do you see in our society that are contrary to the mercy and compassion Jesus speaks about?

FOR PRAYER

God of mercy,
through the death and resurrection of your Son
you have reconciled us to you.
You have sent the Holy Spirit
for the forgiveness of sins.
Grant us pardon and peace.
Touch our hearts that we in our turn
will be merciful to others,
offering them pardon and peace. Amen.

Chapter Nine

'Blessed Are the Pure in Heart' (5:8)

I N OUR MIND'S EYE we picture the man who wrote the Gospel According to Matthew relaxing and enjoying himself as he watches us struggle with the meaning of Jesus' words: "Blessed are the pure in heart, for they will see God." We say, "This seems clear enough. All the words except one are simple monosyllables, and we already have discussed the meaning of the word *blessed*."

Matthew raises a quizzical eye and asks if we really grasp what Jesus meant by the heart and by a pure heart. We respond that we have dismissed the interpretation that understands purity of heart merely as being free of sexual sins. It seems obvious that the words mean more than that. Could they mean that only those who are without sin will get into heaven?

But even as we ask this rhetorical question, the words of John pop into our heads: "If we say that we have no sin, we deceive ourselves, and the truth is not in us" (1 John 1:8). Who is ever completely without sin? The great saints have often thought of themselves as great sinners because they realized that, despite their best efforts, they did not love as completely as Jesus had called them to love. A Beatitude that seems so simple at a quick reading suddenly demands a second and third thoughtful reading.

This kind of reflective reading begins by exploring the connotations of each word, simple as it is. Matthew nods as we begin to wrestle with the meaning of words that we commonly accept without much thought. Challenged, we ask a rhetorical question, "What then did Jesus mean by the word *heart*? He could not have been speaking about the purely physical action of the organ that pumps blood through our veins and capillaries."

With a little reflection we realize that he must have been speaking of the heart as a symbol of the whole person, as the source of both good and evil, as the source of the thoughts and feelings that move people to action. The pure of heart are those whose hearts are not divided, but are centered on God. We might call them the singled-minded. This Beatitude, then, speaks directly about motivation and priorities and only indirectly about action.

When a Pharisee asked Jesus what is the greatest of the commandments, Jesus answered not by saying what a person should or should not do, but by emphasizing the motive that should lie behind all of one's actions: "You shall love the Lord your God with all your heart, and with all your soul, and with all your mind.... You shall love your neighbor as yourself" (see 22:34-39).

We also recall, however, that Jesus said that entrance into the Kingdom depends on "doing" the will of the Father. But this "doing" is more than the act itself. It is a "doing" that is motivated by love for the Father. It is a "doing" that reflects where our treasure is and where our heart lies (see 6:21).

The parable of the two sons who were asked by their father to go and work in the field (21:28-31) illustrates the importance of motivation over words and the fact that our motives are often mixed. The young man said he would gladly go but never did. The other refused, but later changed his mind and went. Even though his motives may have been mixed, his sense of duty and his love for his father overcame his reluctance to work in the field. His duty to his father was in the end his highest priority.

Another young man was a different story. He had kept the commandments, but he was looking for something more. Jesus offered that something more: "[G]o, sell your possessions and give the money to the poor...; then come, follow me" (19:21).

This advice posed a problem for the young man. He had to make a choice. He wanted to do more than keep the commandments, but he also wanted to hang onto the security his possessions gave him. He turned down Jesus' offer and went away sad because he had a divided heart. He was not willing to love God with his whole being.

This narrative highlights the common human problem in focusing all our energies on doing the will of God. Often we are distracted by many other things that seem important but may not be best for our spiritual development.

At times this parable is understood as stating that there are two paths to salvation, one of merely keeping the commandments and a higher one of detachment and following Jesus more perfectly. It really is about the fact that attachment to one's possessions, whatever they are, make it impossible in human terms for a person to enter the Kingdom. The parable points out that concern for one's possessions can come before the call of the Lord. Jesus, however, modified the impact of his words by saying that all things are possible for God (19:26).

A Japanese folk tale about the stonecutter Tasaku illustrates the foolishness of seeking after wealth and power. Tasaku was a poor man who hacked blocks of stone from the foot of a mountain. One day he saw a well-dressed prince ride by. Tasaku envied the prince and wished that he had such wealth and power. A spirit heard him and granted his wish.

Tasaku was happy with his silk clothes and his powerful armies until he saw the sun wilt the flowers in his royal garden. He wished that he had the sun's power.

This wish was also granted. He became the sun with power to parch the fields and cause people to beg for water.

He was happy until a cloud covered him and obscured his powerful heat; then he wanted to be the cloud. The spirit granted his request. Thereafter Tasaku was a cloud with power to ravage the land with storms and floods.

Tasaku was happy until he saw a mountain that stood firm in spite of his storms. And so Tasaku demanded to be a mountain—granted. Tasaku became the mountain. Now he was more powerful than the prince, the sun and the cloud. He was happy until he felt a chisel chipping at his feet. It was a stonecutter working away.

Tasaku had a heart set on something outside himself, power. He did not set his eyes on the finding and loving the One who could satisfy all the desires of his heart. He was single-minded but not pure of heart.

The opposite of a pure heart is a confused heart, one that seeks to have its cake and to eat it, that wants to serve God but at the same time to seek its own pleasure and power. At its hardest it is completely centered on its own desires and neglects the will of the Father entirely. It loves only those who love it (see 5:46). It performs righteous deeds, gives alms or makes a show of its pious deeds in order to be seen and praised by others (see 6:1-6, 16-18).

In very strong language, Jesus denounced the hypocrisy of those who keep the externals of the law without the interior dispositions of a heart that loves God. "Woe to you, scribes and Pharisees, hypocrites! For you clean the outside of the cup and of the plate, but inside they are full of greed and self-indulgence. You blind Pharisee! First clean the inside of the cup, so that the outside also may become clean" (23:25-26).

We wonder why a heart that is centered on God is a "pure heart." Something that is pure is uncontaminated, free of extraneous matter. Obviously, then, a pure heart is one that is free from attachments that do not have to do with the will of the Father.

But if we take this blessing as coming only to those who never do anything except what it is in accord with the will of the Father, we would be hard put to name the recipients. If we take it to mean only those who have no attachment to any kind of sin when they are at the point of death, our list might be longer, but it certainly would not include the vast majority of people.

We ask another very difficult question: "Can anyone ever be so single-minded as to act out of pure, selfless love?" We like to say that we can, but in the last analysis we usually find that our motives are mixed. Perhaps the test for the pure heart that will see God is that God's will is at the top of our priority list even though some selfish motives may be mixed in.

The parable of the three men who were entrusted with varying sums of money by a master who was going off to a far land (25:14-30) helps us see how motives may be mixed and yet still be in the right order. When the master returned home, two of the men had multiplied what he had given them. The third had buried the money and returned it with neither loss nor gain.

The first two put the desire of their master that his wealth increase before their concerns for themselves. They had their priorities in good order. The third put self-preservation before the desire of the master because he knew that the master was hard and the servant was afraid of losing the money.

Perhaps the word *pure* in this Beatitude does not necessarily mean that our motivation in every circumstance is absolutely pure. Even though our primary driving motive is to do all for the greater glory of God, there may be now and then, here and there some minor self-seeking. We say bottled spring water is pure or unadulterated when it has no additives, even though there are mineral traces in it. Twenty-four carat gold is solid gold even though it contains traces of other metals.

Perhaps the purity demanded by this Beatitude is that which comes from having no attachments to serious sins, even though some self-centered desires still remain in our hearts.

Time and time again Jesus spoke in various ways about the need for motivation that goes beyond self-satisfaction. He said that mere words and even good actions do not guarantee that one's motives are pure. He said that he will not acknowledge everyone who says, "Lord, Lord, did we not prophesy in your name, and cast out demons in your name, and do many deeds of power in your name?" (7:21-23). Surely doing these things is not sinful. They do produce happy results in the people who hear and heed the prophesy, who are freed from demons, who are cured of their illnesses. But even these good works can proceed from a heart that is not pure, a heart that is at best divided and at worst completely self-seeking. In the end, what really counts is that heart and action function as one.

A pure heart is characterized by integrity and sincerity. It prompts us to say yes when we mean yes and no when we mean no (see 5:37). It keeps us from passing judgment on others and moves us to work on our own faults before trying to correct those of others (see 7:1-5). It is being simple and trusting in prayer so that we do not babble on like the pagans (see 6:7). Most striking of all it is a forgiving heart (see 6:14).

The desire to get even when we have been hurt, to pile up more riches than we need, to have what belongs to someone else, to satisfy our sexual desires in any way and with anyone, to use drink, drugs or food irresponsibly as well as the inclination to be indifferent to religious practices (especially when they require some effort on our part): All these present serious temptations to the heart that is seeking to center on the will of the Father. When allowed high priority in our lives, these inclinations lead to doing the right thing for the wrong reason. They breed hypocrisy.

A man watched his eighteen-year-old son being

baptized and receiving his first Communion. After the service the father was asked why he did not receive with his son on this important occasion. He responded, "You wouldn't want me to be a hypocrite, would you?" It turned out that he was an alcoholic who he had not been to church in years and was living with a woman not his wife. He understood that participating in Eucharist would be saying something about his intentions that was not true.

His reply raises the question, "What should we do when our interior motives and our priorities are not in line with gospel values?" We can do as that man did and give up any practice that expresses faith, but this does not seem to be the way to the Kingdom. The other option is to change our priorities so that our actions do express the faith and love we profess.

This type of change is not easy. It seldom happens suddenly and at one fell swoop. It takes time and patience. It endures the struggles of life without losing hope. It needs the support of others who are also pure of heart and are intent on following Jesus.

A more pressing question for most of us is, "What can I do when I begin to realize that my motives are mixed and confused?" Becoming pure of heart requires a strong desire to be single-minded. This desire must be united with a faith that recognizes that we are children of God and that our lives are completely in the hands of God. We need trust that God will give the necessary help. We also need to keep asking ourselves questions such as: "Why am I doing this? What do I hope to get out of this? Is this the kind of person I want to be? What does the Lord expect of me?" If we ask these questions of ourselves often enough, we will gradually spot the contaminants in our hearts and rearrange our priorities.

After this long discussion, our friend Matthew seems to be growing a bit impatient, so we look at the final two words of this Beatitude, *see God*. To see God does not mean gazing on the Almighty with our bodily eyes. It means that in our innermost being we will know God, be united with God, love God.

This phrase is the most enticing and the clearest of the promises of happiness attached to the Beatitudes. Nothing will block or blur our vision. No specks or timbers will be in our eyes. We will be one with God. Matthew shakes his head in a way that asks, "Well, what are you going to do about acquiring a pure heart?"

FOR REFLECTION

1) *Is there any value or idea that you have remained single-minded about over the years? Describe how it has influenced your life.*

2) *What are two or three commonly accepted values that make it difficult to be single-minded, pure in heart?*

3) *Someone once said, "The last and greatest treason is to do the right thing for the wrong reason." What would be some of the wrong reasons for doing the right thing?*

FOR PRAYER

Create in me a clean heart, O God,
    and put a new and right spirit within me.
Do not cast me away from your presence,
    and do not take your holy spirit from me.
Restore to me the joy of your salvation,
    and sustain in me a willing spirit....

The sacrifice acceptable to God is a broken
    spirit;
    a broken and contrite heart, O God, you will
    not despise. (Psalm 51:10-12, 17)

Chapter Ten
'Blessed Are the Peacemakers' (5:9)

A S WE SIT TALKING with Matthew we glance out the door and see a squad of Roman legionnaires marching down the road. On the tip of one of their standards is the word *pax*, which means "peace." These are the men who keep order in the Roman Empire. They enforce the *Pax Romana*, the "Roman peace," from one end of the Mediterranean Sea to the other.

These soldiers are peacekeepers, much like the United Nations troops stationed in various parts of the world. They are not present to promote harmony between factions at odds with one another. Their task is to prevent or control violence even if they have to kill in order to stop the killing. Resolving differences and promoting mutual understanding and harmony is the work of diplomats, not soldiers.

Because of these legions, there are few rebellions or civil wars in the Empire. Because they keep bandits and pirates in check, the roads and sea routes connecting the various parts of the Empire are safe for travelers. In a very real way, the Roman world of the first century is a much more peaceful place to live in than our world.

As we watch those seasoned troopers go to their duty posts, we hear the voice of Matthew reading the next

Beatitude: "Blessed are the peacemakers, for they will be called children of God" (5:9). Something in his voice tells us that the peacemakers whom Jesus called children of God do more than keep order by force or negotiate acceptable compromises between people with differing goals. They are those who strive first of all to be at peace with God, to live in harmony with the Lord.

Because they are seeking this inner harmony, they do God-like work. They strive to promote peace in all their relationships and to do what they can to help others, individuals or groups, to live and work together in harmony.

This effort to be a peacemaker is not easy. The peace they strive for is not the gentle disposition which gives way when challenged or the stagnant quiet of inactivity that refuses to do something about difficult situations for the sake of "keeping the peace." Neither is it a false tolerance for whatever others want or do. The peace they strive to achieve is a serenity that permeates all their thinking, all their relationships with others. They also work to promote this same serenity and tranquility in the lives of those they encounter and in society.

"Peace" in the Hebrew Scriptures is *shalom*, a harmony that comes from a right ordering of all one's relationships. *Shalom* embraces God, oneself, others and the world in which we live. True peacemaking is linked with working for justice in the larger society. The Hebrew Scriptures stressed the need to care for the poor, especially widows, orphans and aliens, and to see that all their rights were respected. Peace becomes the fruit of justice when there is a right ordering of relationships, that is, when each person is respected as a child of God.

In the Christian Scriptures peace is first of all a gift from God that comes though a life of prayer and commitment to doing the will of the Lord. Prayer and reflection allow us to face and accept our limitations and our need for physical and emotional care. They bring a calm acceptance of life that enables clear and tranquil thinking.

The challenge of peacemaking lies in being at peace not only with ourselves but also—especially—with our enemies. "But I say to you, Love your enemies and pray for those who persecute you, so that you may be children of your Father in heaven..." (5:44-45). One result of our union with God is that we can approach an enemy not seeking revenge but offering peace, forgiveness and reunion.

Peace is a movement toward the other. It is a movement from resistance to openness, from suspicion to trust, from prejudice to understanding, from division to reconciliation. At the heart of peacemaking is the willingness to forgive and to work with the other. It involves seeking out the other rather than waiting for the other to come to us. It requires courage, openness, trust and patience. Peacemaking takes time.

A young couple had been married about six months before the new bride began to notice that some of her husband's habits annoyed her, especially his practice of never washing his dirty dishes. Every time he had a snack he simply put the dirty dish in the sink. Each time she would grab the dish, wash it and put it away. She said nothing to him for fear of making him angry, but her anger grew daily. In desperation she came up with an idea. She would no longer wash his dishes.

After a few days all the dishes were piled up in the sink. Finally she felt she had to say something to him. She carefully planned what and how to say it and waited for the right moment. Then she said, "When you eat a snack and put your dish in the sink, it makes me angry because I have to wash it."

He replied in a surprised voice, "But I thought you liked washing dishes. You're always doing them." She burst out laughing at the thought that she liked to do dishes. He agreed to wash his dishes after snacking. Peace was restored in their home.

Making peace brings new and better relationships with others. It helps us put hurts behind us and see the other person in a new way. It deepens our trust in ourselves and in others. The heart of this Beatitude is a call to deal creatively with conflict, knowing that at times this will not be easy.

This call to be creative brings to mind a question: "What are the tools, the weapons, the means we have to be peacemakers?" They certainly are not anger, violence, fear or force. Those who strive to bring the Lord's peace rely on charity coupled with hope. Love shown by the listening heart, the soft-spoken word, the kind deed, the recognized concern opens hardened hearts to the peace of God. Hope shown by the concerned effort to understand lays the ground for mutual understanding. Prayer, patience, wisdom, knowledge, courage and perseverance all are needed in various ways and at different times by the peacemaker who seeks to restore unity where discord is present.

The attitudes enunciated by the Beatitudes are the most effective guides we have in our efforts to bring about peace.

1) Being poor in spirit, that is, recognizing our absolute dependence on God, helps us recognize that peace in any situation depends more on God than on our efforts. We do our best, but are comfortable with the realization that there is no easy victory when hearts are set in opposition to one another.

2) Mourning over our weakness, false pride and sinfulness helps us to be conscious of these failings in others and to empathize with all the parties.

3) Having a meek (not wishy-washy!) spirit helps us

keep our temper and control our anger when others get angry with us or frustrate us.

4) Hungering and thirsting for justice motivates us to help people in their efforts to be right with God and to live in harmony with one another.

5) Having a pure heart focuses our energy on aiding the work of God by bringing individuals and groups to live and work together harmoniously.

6) Having a merciful and compassionate heart impels us to forgive and to urge others to forgive and to try to live in peace.

The next question that comes to mind is, "Where am I called to be a peacemaker? I can't do anything about civil wars in places like Bosnia or about gang warfare in our cities. I don't feel that my efforts will contribute much to alleviating the tensions in the Church. People I know are estranged, but nothing I have to say helps the situation." All this may be true, but each of us is nevertheless called to foster peace to the best of our ability in situations we encounter each day.

Most of us must daily struggle for that complete and true inner peace that comes only when all our energies are concentrated on God, the ultimate goal, and when our hearts are undisturbed by other attractions. We are challenged by events to bring peace into our own lives by quelling the civil war going on within us. On one side are the tendencies that constantly try to push the will of God more to the periphery of our lives and to move our will into the center. These destructive tendencies are called the capital sins: an inflated pride of self, envy, greed, anger, lust, spiritual laziness and gluttony. On the other side are the good habits or virtues that defend God's position as Lord of our lives.

Besides this effort to foster inner peace, we also are

challenged to make peace with those who may be estranged from us or from whom we feel estranged. "So when you are offering your gift at the altar, if you remember that your brother has something against you, leave your gift there before the altar and go; first be reconciled with your brother or sister, and then come and offer your gift" (5:23-24). The implication of this saying is that God is much more pleased with a peacemaking heart than with any other gift people can offer.

For that reason we are expected to leave our gifts at the altar and seek reconciliation with someone against whom we carry a grudge or harbor anger. How God looks upon those who refuse to be reconciled is brought out in the parable following this saying: The judge will be severe with those who do not settle their differences quickly (5:25-26). It is not too difficult to identify people in our family or among our friends with whom we have had a disagreement, a quarrel or even a fight. Each of these situations calls for us to be the peacemaker. We need to be willing to put aside our pride and our desire for justice or revenge and make the first overtures, opening our hearts to what the other is trying to say, not merely to what we think the other is saying.

What we can do to make peace between individuals who are quarreling or estranged depends completely on the circumstances. Often we can do nothing except pray for the parties. At other times a wise word, a loving gesture, a listening ear, even a stern admonition will move the parties to begin to work out their differences. Love, hope and patience are needed in all cases.

The hardest challenge we face is how to be a peacemaker in society. The divisions between groups are so deep that we can easily throw up our hands and retreat behind the walls of our home. Yet there are always some people or some groups we can join or at least financially support who are striving to bring peace through justice.

FOR REFLECTION

1) *What inner qualities or feelings do you associate with being at peace with yourself and with being at peace with others?*

2) *Recall a time when you were a peacemaker. Which of the attitudes expressed in the Beatitudes were helpful in your efforts?*

3) *What practical steps could you take to foster peace in one of the areas of our society that need healing?*

FOR PRAYER

Lord, make me an instrument of your peace.
Where there is hatred, let me sow love.
where there is injury, pardon;
where there is doubt, faith;
where there is despair, hope;
where there is darkness, light;
and where there is sadness, joy.
O Divine Master,
grant that I may not so much seek
to be consoled as to console;
to be understood, as to understand;
to be loved, as to love.
For it is in giving that we receive,
it is pardoning that we are pardoned,
it is in dying that we are born to eternal life.
                    (attributed to St. Francis of Assisi)

Chapter Eleven

'Blessed Are Those Who Are Persecuted' (5:10-11)

W E READ THE LAST BEATITUDE and wonder why Matthew doubles this Beatitude about persecution. He said it clearly enough the first time: "Blessed are those who are persecuted for righteousness' sake, for theirs is the kingdom of heaven" (5:10). But then he repeats it in a slightly different form: "Blessed are you when people revile you and persecute you..." (see 5:11-12).

One obvious answer is that Matthew had at hand two slightly different sayings of Jesus about the persecution his followers will face and uses both of them. Luke phrases it in still another way: "Blessed are you when people hate you, and when they exclude you and revile you and defame you on account of the Son of Man" (Luke 6:22).

Jesus must have spoken in slightly different words many times about mercy, sorrow for sin, being poor in spirit, being a peacemaker. Why did Matthew not see fit to couple the other Beatitudes with an amplifying verse? We can only guess at his reasons. One reason would seem to be that he was offering encouragement and hope to a people who were facing either some type of persecution or imminent danger of it. It is relatively easy to understand how people who are merciful, single-minded or peacemakers will enjoy a certain peace and satisfaction even here on earth. It is extremely difficult to comprehend how a person can find peace and joy in being rejected, insulted, calumniated, jailed, stoned, tortured or killed.

By repeating this blessing, Matthew seems to be saying that Jesus knew how difficult it would be to follow him. Jesus had said he had come not to bring peace but the sword, to put father and son, daughter and mother, daughter-in-law and mother-in-law at odds with each other because of him (see 10:34-36). He had said that this opposition could be so strong that brother would hand over brother and father would hand over his child to death and that children would rise up against their parents because of him (see 10:21-22).

Most likely, Matthew knew how the followers of Jesus were already being persecuted and he wanted to offer them reassurance and hope. He knew what had happened to the prophets of old and to John the Baptist. He surely recounted to his community what had happened to Jesus on Good Friday.

Although he had no fax or e-mail, information about the persecutions various Christians were undergoing would have spread by letter and courier quickly throughout the network of believing communities. Luke had not yet written the Acts of the Apostles, but Matthew must have heard of the stoning of Stephen, the first persecutions of the Church, the beheading of James as well as of the trials of Paul and of the martyrdom of Peter and Paul in Rome just a few years before he wrote his Gospel. Believers had to realize that such problems were inherent in being a Christian and not a sign that all was finished.

The only way we can rejoice and be glad and feel blessed when suffering any sort of persecution is by having our eyes fixed on something better to come. The reward Jesus promises to those who are faithful takes our breath away: "Everyone therefore who acknowledges me before others, I also will acknowledge before my Father in heaven" (10:32).

Imagine standing before the judgment seat of God with all your sins, failings and imperfections and Jesus standing next to you, saying, "Joe [Jane] is OK. He [she] stood up for me." On the other hand, imagine being in that same situation and hearing Jesus say to his heavenly Father, "This one denied me before others!" (see 10:32-33).

We would then grasp what Jesus meant when he said, "Those who find their life will lose it, and those who lose their life for my sake will find it" (10:39).

All the Beatitudes promise a reward in the next life, in the kingdom that is to come. It is not too difficult to see how the other seven Beatitudes also offer in this life a foretaste of the peace and closeness to God that will be ours in the eternal kingdom. It is extremely difficult to see that being hated and excluded—much less being jailed or killed—offers those rewards. If we do not have hope for something better to come out of our suffering and even out of our death, we have been taken in by one of the greatest hoaxes in history.

If we accept the premise that persecution is a condition for a great reward in heaven, the obvious question is whether we will get little or no reward if we face little or no persecution for the sake of Jesus. We know of people throughout history who have died for their faith. We have read of people in places like communist Russia, Nazi Germany, Central or South America who in recent decades have been imprisoned, tortured or killed because of their faith. But we live in a country that upholds freedom of religion along with separation of Church and state.

It is true that there have been in this country instances of bigotry and outright violence against people

87

because of their fidelity to Jesus, but these have been the exception, not the rule. For the most part the biggest threat that the followers of Jesus face here is not violence but indifference. The message vibrant Christians bring and the life-style they promote are seen by more and more people to be irrelevant. This is a form of persecution in itself. Being ignored when we are deeply committed to a person or a cause is often more painful than outright physical violence.

But the question still remains: Is the blessing limited to those who are beaten, jailed or killed for an ideal? That would be too superficial an understanding of what Jesus was calling for. Not everyone who is persecuted for an ideal is automatically promised a place in the Kingdom. People can suffer persecution because they are misguided, motivated by pride or even because they have a martyr complex.

The attitude that deserves this blessing is closely allied to being single-hearted. It is fidelity to Jesus and his way of life. It is a firm stance in this commitment. It is an openness to the possibility that we will be persecuted in some way—perhaps in a physically violent manner but probably in some more subtle way. The values of Jesus are in direct opposition to those of the world; to act on his values will often bring turmoil and suffering into our lives. We may be shunned or discriminated against or just called fools, but we will feel rejection. This Beatitude expresses a willingness to accept persecution in any form when it comes.

Willingness to accept persecution is not merely passive resignation to the inevitable. In the spirit of the other Beatitudes, this acceptance comes from a humble attitude that recognizes that if the Master suffered, so too must we. It is a spirit that forgives and prays for the persecutors. It is a spirit motivated by the desire to keep our relationship with God whole and intact, one that hopes peace and understanding will emerge from our suffering.

Thus, not everyone who is persecuted or oppressed will automatically be assured of a place in the Kingdom. Nor are those who do not suffer some form of overt persecution automatically denied a high place in the Kingdom. The blessing comes to those who willingly maintain in the face of all obstacles fidelity to their relationship with Jesus. "[Y]ou will be hated by all.... But the one who endures to the end will be saved" (10:22).

Actually, this willingness is tested more often than we realize by situations in which we are called upon to stand up for a gospel value. In these situations *persecution* may seem too strong a word. Perhaps *tested* is a more realistic expression. Most of us will be tested frequently by some opposition from family and those close to us when we are trying to live according to the gospel.

The challenge is rarely to our beliefs about God or Jesus but often to the values that flow from those beliefs. Do I stand up for my faith or for the truth when someone is mocking or attacking it? Do I speak out when I hear racial jokes or unkind judgments or keep quiet because I fear what people will think or say to me? Do I go along with the crowd because everyone is doing it? Am I willing to be a whistle-blower when I see something dishonest in my place of employment? Do I turn my back on an injustice because it is easier not to get involved? These are some of the challenges we meet that can lead to persecution of a less serious kind than jail or death.

In the Roman persecutions of the first three centuries and in the communist and Nazi persecutions, faithful Christians were sent to prison and even to death not because they believed in Jesus, but because they put God above Caesar and were seen as a threat to the state. So, too, in our country today, we will be laughed at, insulted and mocked not so much for believing in Jesus but for standing up for gospel values.

We will be dismissed as ignorant of the way the world really works when we try to promote ethically and socially responsible business practices. We will be told that business is business and that religion is something else. We will be put down with the assurance that the Church should stay out of politics when we speak up on issues such as abortion, euthanasia and help to the needy, even illegal immigrants. Accusations of being old-fashioned will be leveled at us for upholding premarital chastity or for believing that marriage is a lifelong commitment, for better or for worse. We will be seen as living in a dream world if we turn our backs on the materialism and consumerism of our age. We may even go to jail for protesting against nuclear weapons or abortion on demand.

The threats to our commitment to Jesus today very seldom come from fire or sword. They come from the people around us. But most often they come from a most pernicious persecutor, the self-centered inclinations that lurk in our hearts. These insidious foes of Christ take many forms in their efforts to keep us from being faithful to our commitment. They counsel us to play it safe, to turn our eyes in another direction, to be neutral when we see blatant injustice. They suggest that for the sake of harmony it is best to keep quiet when we see people acting in destructive ways. The virus of anger may urge us to protect our rights by violence or by confrontations that violate charity.

The desire to be in with the "right" people, to be accepted and respected, may nudge us to keep quiet about gospel values. The fear of losing a job or of endangering our security may seal our lips about an unethical business practice. One of the worst interior persecutors is a lack of trust that God is in charge and that Jesus is with us no matter how difficult the situation is. If our faith is not merely lip service, we are tormented by the doubts these desires and fears bring about. Our interior peace is disrupted because we sense what we should do and do not have the courage to do it.

These inner inclinations to escape the less violent forms of persecution are aspects of the cross that Jesus said must be taken up by those who wish to follow him (16:24). In order to recognize them for what they are, an effort to cause us to deny Christ, we need to name them and recognize how we usually react to them. We need the kind of faith that will impel us to step out of the boat like Peter and walk on water because we believe that Jesus is with us in all situations. And we need to pray for help to face them willingly.

Reflecting on questions such as the following help us identify how well the attitudes called for by this Beatitude operate in our hearts. Pick one or two that seem most true about you and spend some time praying about them.

1) How do I feel when I feel that I have been ignored, belittled, dismissed for a position I take because I see it as a Christian value?

2) What is my reaction to the people whom I see doing these things to me? Do I grow angry, ignore them, strike out physically?

3) When people hold a position opposite to mine, do I show them understanding, willingness to listen and perhaps to change or modify my position?

4) Do I presume goodwill on the part of those who disagree with my ideas about how gospel values are to be put into action? Or do I use harsh, judgmental words in speaking to or of them?

5) Do I forgive those whom I feel have in some way oppressed or persecuted me or do I harbor resentful thoughts and feelings toward them? Do I pray for them?

6) In what situations am I the persecutor? Do I

dismiss, reject, mock, insult those who do not go along with my ideas, my values and especially my solutions to problems?

FOR REFLECTION

1) *Why would Christianity be the greatest hoax ever perpetrated on the human race if there is no heaven and no judgment?*

2) *Can you recall a situation in which you suffered some type of discrimination or rejection because you upheld a gospel value?*

3) *Can you recall a time when you were tempted to be silent or to act contrary to a gospel value because of the opposition you faced from others?*

FOR PRAYER

Lord, you suffered death on the cross
for love of us.
Please give us the courage
to endure the small sufferings of this life
for love of you. Amen.

Chapter Twelve

'Salt of the Earth' and 'Light of the World' (5:13-16)

W E SET THE SCROLL DOWN, lean back and sigh. Looking at Matthew sitting quietly across from us we say, "You have given us much to think about. These words of Jesus challenge our comfortable way of being Christian. We have tried to keep the commandments. We do love God. We help the poor. We believe in the Beatitudes even if we do not work too hard on developing the attitudes they express. It's not easy, but we are trying."

Matthew nods. He understands what we are trying to say, but a sly grin creeps into his face. He asks, "Why are you trying to do all these things?"

Surprised we answer, "Because we believe, of course. We want to be good followers of Christ. We want to save our souls. We want to get to heaven."

Matthew responds, "All good reasons, but can you think of another reason why these eight ways of walking in the way of the Lord are so important in your life?"

"What can be as important as keeping the commandments, loving our neighbor and saving our soul?" we ask.

"Who can say which motive is more important in guiding a person to the Kingdom? But if you read a few lines further on you will discover a very important reason why we are called to be humble, meek, merciful, hungry for righteousness, clean of heart, peacemakers and willing to suffer persecution," Matthew responds.

We run our eyes over the next few lines and two words catch our eyes. "You are the *salt* of the earth.... You are the *light* of the world" (5:13-16).

"Good!" Matthew replies, "How can you be the salt of the earth and the light of the world except by putting the Beatitudes into practice? Think about it."

Taking Matthew at his word, we recall pictures of people who have shed light in the darkness of this world and who have put zest back into the lives of people who were lost and discouraged. We recall the great saints who worked miracles, the great missionaries who labored to bring entire nations to Christ as well as the famous preachers who inspired thousands to change their way of life.

"Stop! Stop!" Matthew cries. "Look at the first word in each of those sentences. It is *you!*"

We realize that these two admonitions are addressed to all the followers of Christ, not to just a few. They are addressed to each of us individually and to all of us collectively. They sum up the mission of the disciples: to reach out to others.

A light left burning in a room with no one in it does nothing but use up electricity. Salt sitting in a shaker on the table or contaminated by some other substance is of no help to anyone. Both light and salt need to be in contact with people if they are to carry out their purpose. Just so, the one who says, "I believe," needs to touch the lives of others in order to be a true disciple of the Lord. Preaching the message is important, but this reaching out and touching is most effective when it flows from the attitudes encapsulated in the Beatitudes.

Salt and light are such common elements that we cannot easily conceive of life without them. Even though they are common, we appreciate what they contribute to our lives. Salt keeps food from spoiling. Food is flat and bland, even tasteless, without salt. Just the right amount of salt enhances the flavor and enjoyment of our food. It takes a blackout to make us appreciate the importance of light in our lives. Light, even the small light of a flashlight, prevents us from stumbling over furniture or other objects in the dark. It helps us find our way whether we are in the house or out on the road. At times a light warns us of danger, illuminating a dangerous path or flashing red at a crossing. At other times it is a warm, welcoming sign— like a porch light at the house where the party is.

The light which touches our eyes and helps us see where we are and what surrounds us is only a faint comparison to the light Jesus was speaking about. Jesus himself is the light of the world that transforms everything around him. At his Transfiguration (17:2) the disciples saw Jesus, the place they were, the Law, the Prophets and themselves in an entirely different manner than they had understood them before.

Disciples who try to live by the vision and the attitudes expressed in the Beatitudes reflect this light from Jesus. They, too, are transformed. The quality of their lives transforms the world around them. They show the way and by their example encourage others to walk on that way.

The parable Jesus told about the wise and the foolish virgins (25:1-13) gives us an insight into how we are to care for the light that has been entrusted to us. The bridesmaids were to wait at the house of the groom to welcome him and the bride, but no one knew exactly when they would arrive. The groom had to negotiate a price for the bride. The longer the delay, the greater the compliment paid to the bride. It indicated that she was very precious and that the groom had to pay dearly as the bride's father held out for a high price.

Wise bridesmaids brought enough oil for their lamps to last through a long wait. To run out of oil was a disaster and a sign of disrespect toward the bride and groom and their entourage. We are called to be wise bridesmaids, torches alight with faith and good works, waiting to welcome the Bridegroom and his friends.

One strong-minded woman made no bones about being an atheist. In fact, she denied the existence of God whenever she had a chance. One day she entered a hospital for a serious operation. The night before she was to go under the knife, a sister came into her hospital room and listened to her fears. The sister said very little, but her calmness and concern helped relieve the tension the woman felt.

Next morning before the operation, the sister came again, walked beside the gurney to the operating room and held the woman's hand until she lost consciousness. When the woman awoke after the operation, the sister was sitting beside her, stroking her forehead.

When the atheist left the hospital she told her friends about the sister who had been so kind to her. "If this is what faith in God does for a person, then I think I'm ready for conversion." The sister was a peacemaker for a frightened woman, poor in spirit (read humble and meek) with a woman who relied totally on herself, merciful to someone in need. She was light in that woman's life.

As we mull over the symbolism of these two words, *light* and *salt*, we gradually begin to see how appropriate they are when applied to the tasks facing Jesus' disciples today. Salt has a particular relevance for our efforts at renewal within the Church. It is easy to recognize that many Christians follow Jesus in a half-hearted, routine manner. Their faith life has little fervor and is not high on their list of priorities. In every age, particularly in a climate of rapid change such as we live in, there is a great need for renewal within the community of believers. The need to be renewed is not restricted only to the wishy-washy Christians. There is a need for every disciple to fire up enthusiasm for the Lord.

In the Church today many efforts add zest to the faith life of active members. The many ministries now open to laypeople, as well as RENEW groups, small faith communities, Bible study groups, prayer groups, Christian Initiation and programs for those who are returning to a more active participation are all aimed at stirring up the banked fire of the Holy Spirit in our hearts.

Nevertheless, all these groups fall far short of Jesus' admonition to be salt and light in the world if they concentrate all their energy on the development of their members and do not lead them to reach out to others. A disciple needs to be seasoned with the salt of the Spirit but also to be light for those who wander in darkness.

This other symbol, light, is an apt image of the evangelizing efforts of the Church. The Church community is that city of light on a mountain that attracts people to come in and stay. The Church, both institutionally and individually, has to reach out and share the light that is Christ with those who walk in the darkness. This darkness envelopes not only those who see no need for religion or who do not know Christ, but also also those who have been handed a candle at Baptism as a sign of the light of faith but who do not fully know or appreciate the Christian faith.

The evangelizing task of the Church is also the task of every disciple. All are called to bring the light of Christ to the people they encounter at work, in the shops, in their neighborhood, on the highway and even at the car wash. The questions for most of us are, "How often have we talked about our faith with another? How often have we invited someone to learn more about the faith?"

A priest tells of asking a man who had been coming to Mass for several years why he had never become a Catholic. The man said, "No one has asked me." All the people in his circle of friends were Catholic. The priest said, "I'm asking you now." The man said "OK," and was baptized some time later. It is true that many people evangelize in a quiet way, but more open and understanding individual approaches are needed.

We look at Matthew and ask, "Why didn't you give us a clear job description for being a disciple instead of dropping hints here and there of what is required?" As usual, he smiles and says, "Because Jesus only gave a very general commission. For example, to the man whose name I bear all he said was, 'Follow me' (9:9). I imagine that it took him many years to find out all that was involved in following Jesus. If you look at Jesus' commissioning of the Twelve, however, I think you will find a general outline of what a disciple is expected to do to spread the Good News."

We look though chapter ten and pick out some of Jesus' expectations of the Twelve. But, since Matthew never seems to make a great distinction between the Twelve and the other disciples, we surmise that all the words are intended for all of us.

The first injunction,"Go nowhere among the Gentiles and enter no town of the Samaritans, but go rather to the lost sheep of the house of Israel" (10:5-6), obviously was meant just for those first missionaries. We need to understand the commission in the light of Jesus' last words to the Eleven: "Go therefore and make disciples of all nations, baptizing them in the name of the Father and of the Son and of the Holy Spirit, and teaching them to obey everything that I have commanded you" (28:19-20). It is obvious that we can exclude no group, no culture, no nation from the missionary efforts of the Church.

The individual must look around and see who in his or her environment needs to hear the message. But this search also requires us to think of the best way to present the message that the Kingdom is at hand. People often have no expectation of a coming kingdom or have a very distorted idea of what it will be like.

The second injunction is to "cure the sick, raise the dead, cleanse the lepers, cast out demons" (10:8). If we take these words too literally most of us will feel that we are excused because we can't work miracles. This list of instructions can be understood in a symbolic way: We are to help people in any way we can and in so doing bring healing to them body and soul.

The third injunction, not to depend on money and not to look for comfort, is a hard one for us today. An underlying tenet of our society is that with money you can achieve anything you wish. We tend to think that this premise also applies to spreading the gospel. Missions need to be supported. Missionaries need to live. Programs need to be financed. The underlying message of Jesus' injunction is that the success of our work will depend more on God's providence and help than on our careful planning for the future and dependence on sufficient material resources (10:9-15).

Next Jesus gives his friends the good news that they will not always be welcomed. In fact, he says that one mark of a disciple will be opposition and persecution in some form. But they are not to allow that to hinder them because he, Jesus, will stand up for them before the throne of God (10:16-33). They will receive the same kind of reception that Jesus did: Some people accepted him, others ignored him, still others rejected him and one group finally plotted to kill him. If one does not bear the cross that the mission entails, that person is not worthy to be called a disciple (10:37-39; 16:24-28).

It would be easy to shrug off these words as applying to the chosen few, such as the successors of the apostles, but in some way they apply in the life of each one of us. A million questions about how each of us is supposed to follow these injunctions of Jesus rise in our minds. We look to Matthew for help, but he seems to be getting ready to leave. We open our mouth to ask and he says, "I know what you are going to ask. Don't ask. Figure it out for yourself in company with other believers."

FOR REFLECTION

1) *Describe someone who is or who has been either light or salt in your life.*

2) *In what way have you been either salt or light to another?*

3) *What evangelizing efforts are being made in your parish or diocese? In which have you participated?*

4) *Which of these characteristics of a disciple do you find to be most difficult? Why?*

FOR PRAYER

Jesus, we believe.
Stir up in our hearts
the flame of enthusiasm
for you and your mission
and give us the help we need
to work for renewal
and to work at evangelization. Amen.

Chapter Thirteen
Alms, Prayer, Fasting (6:1-18)

OUR INTERVIEW OF MATTHEW has been going on for some hours. Now we sit in silence, not sure how to proceed. We sit contemplating the man who has written this incredibly profound book. We are struck with the peace that seems to radiate from his presence. At times he says little, but we sense that he is in the presence of someone who has captured his heart and mind. To ask Matthew what he is thinking or how he came to be at one with himself would break the spirit of this beautiful moment. We have the impression that this is what a life that has been reformed in the light of Christ is like.

It seems clear that Matthew has grasped what it means to follow Jesus. In our time with him, we have noticed that he is always warm, open to our presence, ever ready to respond to our questions. He has patiently and gently opened our eyes to the vision of Jesus and his way of life. Matthew truly embodies what it means to be a disciple of the Lord. He is one who has come in contact with Jesus either in person or through those who personally knew Jesus and has learned his humble and gentle ways.

At last we get up the courage to break the spell and ask Matthew to share the secret of the inner strength and peace he has found. After a long pause he responds with one word: "Surrender." Seeing the puzzled look on our faces, he continues, "Surrender to his way of life, surrender to his vision and put his word into practice."

Before we ask just how we surrender to Jesus' vision and way of life, we ponder what is implied by that word. The difficulty of letting go of our way of life, of what we value, is illustrated by a story about a Japanese soldier, Lieutenant Hiro Onada, who refused to surrender after World War II until he had wasted half of his life. On December 27, 1944, he had been sent to defend a tiny six-by eight-mile island in the Philippines against an impending American invasion. The battle was short and fierce. Most of the Japanese soldiers were killed on the first day. Within a short time the American forces moved on, unaware that a few Japanese soldiers were still hiding in the jungle.

Within six months six of them surrendered to the authorities. By April 1946 only four were left in hiding. In 1949 only three were still alive. This number was reduced to two, Onada and a companion, by 1954. Eighteen years later, in 1972, Onada's companion died and he was alone. Two years of loneliness and despair finally brought Onada out of the jungle to surrender. Thirty years earlier he had heard the Americans' call to surrender because the war was over, but he had not believed it. He had been certain that the Emperor would never give in. He had refused to accept the truth that hostilities had ended and that he was free to go home.

Surrendering one's certainties and being open to a new possibility is always difficult. It implies that we have to let go of that which brought security in the past and give control of our life and of our future to someone or something new. Entrusting our life to an unknown future always involves some suffering and self-denial. It is not easy!

Matthew seems to be reading our thoughts. He softly

reminds us that surrendering to the Lord is not something we do all at once. It is a process that takes place over a period of time, often a long and difficult process. Then he indicates three short passages in his Gospel that are the basis of all Christian spirituality: almsgiving (6:1-4), prayer (6:5-14) and fasting (6:16-18). These three practices are the tools that help us surrender to the Lord. When they are done for the right motive and with the right attitude they will slowly but surely transform us into salt for the earth and light for the world.

Almsgiving (6:1-4)

Why are charitable donations so important in developing one's closeness to the Lord? One reason is that our alms help God's other children who are suffering and in need. Our gifts feed and clothe Christ, who is in the least of his brothers and sisters (24:40). The other is that letting go of our material possessions frees us from worry about them and opens our hearts to God's transforming grace. It overcomes the temptation to build up our stocks, bonds, bank accounts and material possessions. Generous almsgiving counters the inclination to greed and envy in our hearts. Every time we give generously and quietly, we are putting our trust for the future in the Lord.

What is the right way to give money or possessions to help the poor? It has to be done not merely from a humanitarian motive but from a religious one, from a desire to show gratitude to God and to show our trust in God's provident care. The gift is given to honor God and as such it is to be given quietly and without fanfare, without a plaque on the wall, a name on a building or a mention in the newspaper. One hand is not to let the other know what it is doing (6:3-4).

How much we are to give is another story. Each of us must make up his or her own mind. In the story about the rich young man who came to Jesus asking what he needed to do to be saved, Jesus did not tell him to give away all but the possessions he needed in order to live. He told him to sell all that he had, give it to the poor and then come and follow him (19:16-22).

This command of a once-and-for-all surrender of one's possessions is drastic. Saint Basil once said that the excess wealth of the rich is the property of the poor and that the failure to give alms is tantamount to theft. Saint Ambrose of Milan affirmed that wealth beyond one's needs belongs to those who lack necessities. A few saints have taken the Lord's word to the young man literally and disposed of all they had in one generous gesture. Most followers of Christ hear it and gradually give more and more to help the poor. They continually question whether they might be able to give a little more.

Cardinal Bernardin tells in his book, *The Gift of Peace*, that it was only a few years before he had to face his coming death that he finally gave away the stocks and bonds he had set aside for an emergency and decided to put all his trust in the Lord.

The Christian community helps its members in this regard. In apostolic times it organized the distribution of food by the Church at Jerusalem (Acts 6:1-6). Through its organized fund drives, the Church today quietly and without trumpet blasts helps the poor, the hungry, the homeless, the sick and those affected by natural disasters.

Fasting (6:16-18)

We ask Matthew about fasting: "Why did Jesus emphasize abstaining from food and drink?" He answers that Jesus accepted the Jewish practice of fasting as a way of showing humility before God and as a means of obtaining divine favor. But Jesus talked about the *manner* in which one should fast. The penance should not be done

with outward signs that tell the whole world that one is
fasting. It should be done quietly and be primarily a
fasting of the heart, an abstaining from those things that
distance us from the Lord. The prophet Joel said it well,
"[R]end your hearts and not your clothing./Return to the
LORD, your God..." (Joel 2:13).

Matthew's words cause us to reflect a bit on why we
fast and on how fasting opens the heart to the gifts of
God. Fasting (that includes all forms of penance) is similar
to almsgiving because it purifies the mind for
contemplation and communion with God. The hunger we
feel when we fast makes us conscious of our sins and
faults as well as of our need to hunger and thirst for
justice. Instead of being an inconvenience, it should be a
call to hunger for and to seek a closer union with God.

Studies have shown that fasting does clear the mind
and body, making it easier to reach out to God in prayer.
Fasting goes hand in hand with almsgiving. As we deny
ourselves food or drink, we should be motivated to reach
out to those who are in need. Pope Paul VI recommended
that fasting be accompanied by prayers and works of
charity.

Prayer (6:5-8)

Regular prayer helps disciples keep in the forefront
of their minds the ultimate purpose of what they are
doing: namely, the honor and glory of God. The prayer of
which Jesus spoke was a quiet, unostentatious union with
the Father. We read what Jesus had to say about prayer
and ask, "Surely he was not intending that all praying
should be done in secret by ourselves."

There is no need for Matthew to reply, because he
has recorded that Jesus went to the synagogue and to the
Temple at the prescribed times. It would seem obvious
that as a devout Jew he prayed the *Shema* morning and

evening and that he said the *Shemoneh 'eseh* during the day. But Jesus words are directed at the way one prays. There is no need to pile up words.

A priest once gave a talk on the letters of Paul. After the talk, one of the listeners asked, "Father, shouldn't we give thanks?" "Oh yes," the priest said and lifted his arms and his eyes to heaven and said a heartfelt, "Thanks." As he walked out of the hall he saw the man and his friends huddled in a circle giving a much more wordy thanks to the Lord.

Jesus was warning against saying our private prayers so that other people will notice us praying and praise us as holy people. Another priest was criticized by one of the people present at a meeting for not praying at its beginning and at its end. He asked her how many times she had prayed during the meeting. She replied, "How could I? You did not give me time to say a prayer." He told her, "I prayed silently at least three times during that meeting for the help we needed to move on."

Jesus's warnings ring a bell for us. It is so easy to repeat time after time the same formula without thinking of what the words mean—and, more importantly, without the sentiments or attitudes reflected in the words. It is so easy to impute a magical quality to a set formula said at a set time in a set place as though God is not everyplace and does not know our needs. It is easy to confuse verbosity with piety and fluency with devotion. When we go into a quiet space by ourselves and reach out to our Father like a little child, we do not need many words. We do need trust, love, attention.

Our motto for prayer ought to be, "Less not more," meaning that we take time to reflect on the meaning of the words we are saying and on the sentiments we are trying to express. There are many forms of prayer. There are communal and private prayers. There are prayers that require the use of words and others that require us to be silent. There are formal prayers and informal ones. There are many different forms of meditation. No one can be expected to practice them all. We need to experiment until we find the form of prayer most helpful in bringing us into union with God. We do, however, need to practice some form of prayer daily.

These three disciplines—charitable donations, fasting and prayer—help us let go of our narrow perspectives and focus directly on God present in the depths of our hearts. They must be done in secret, known to God alone. In this way they will not become a source of pride and praise from others. The peaceful and caring behavior that results from them will be a sign to others of God's concern for them and a sign that our hearts belong to God alone. Then they may sense in us what we sensed in Matthew: the secret of surrendering to Jesus and to the Good News he brings.

Our private musings have caused us mentally to drift away from Matthew's presence. He stirs and apologizes because he has to leave soon and move on to the next bookstore. We ask him to stay a bit longer and before he goes to help us look at the way the Lord told his disciples to pray.

FOR REFLECTION

1) *From what you have read so far in the Gospel, what is your impression of the man called Matthew who wrote it?*

2) *Recall a time when you had to surrender some idea or position that was important to you and you found something richer and better.*

3) *What are some of the problems you experience in almsgiving?*

4) *When you fast, what benefit do you get from the practice? What keeps you from fasting on a more regular basis?*

5) What is your favorite form of prayer? Why?

FOR PRAYER

Father,
you have taught us to overcome our sins
by prayer, fasting and works of mercy.
When we are discouraged by our weakness,
give us confidence in your love.

We ask this through our Lord Jesus Christ, your
   Son,
who lives and reigns with you and the Holy
   Spirit,
one God, for ever and ever. Amen.
      (Opening Prayer for the Third Sunday of Lent)

Chapter Fourteen

The Lord's Prayer, Part One (6:9-10)

M ATTHEW BEGINS TO PACK up his things, getting ready to move on to the next book signing. We get ready to come back to our own century, but before we part, we ask, "Didn't Jesus say more about how to pray?" Matthew stops putting his books away, looks at us and asks, "What more is there to say that is not in the prayer he gave his disciples? It is all there."

The Our Father is one of those prayers we learn from our parents as little children. We say it often by ourselves and also with others, especially when we gather as a family at the eucharistic table. It burrows deep into our minds and hearts. It sustains us in times of need.

Like this: A woman lay dying in the hospital. She had been in a coma for three days and had given no response to anyone who visited her. The pastor came and sat by her bed. Gently he greeted her, saying her name. She gave no response. After a short time he took her hand and asked her to pray with him. He began slowly, "Our Father, who art in heaven, hallowed be thy name." At these words she slowly opened her eyes. He continued, "Thy kingdom come. Thy will be done on earth as it is in heaven." At this she looked at him, squeezed his hand and smiled. He paused for a moment, and then she began the next phrase, "Give us this day our daily bread" and continued to say the prayer with him to the end. After she had completed the prayer she closed her eyes and slipped back into a coma. These were the last words she said before she died.

Later her pastor said, "The words seemed to come from the depth of her soul. It was as if she was waiting for someone to begin the prayer so she could put herself in the hands of God, as she had done each day of her life. With these words she was able to move with faith and confidence into eternity with God."

Pick up Matthew's Gospel and once again read those familiar words:

> Our Father in heaven,
> hallowed be your name.
> Your kingdom come.
> Your will be done,
> on earth as it is in heaven.
> Give us today our daily bread.
> And forgive us our debts,
> as we also have forgiven our debtors.
> And do not bring us to the time of trial,
> but rescue us from the evil one. (6:9-13)

We wonder why the same prayer is found in a shorter form in Luke:

> Father, hallowed be your name.
> Your kingdom come.
> Give us each day our daily bread.
> And forgive us our sins,
> for we ourselves forgive
> everyone indebted to us.
> And do not bring us
> to the time of trial. (Luke 11:2-4)

Jesus must have spoken often about the way to pray. He well may have used slightly different words when he did. Perhaps two different versions were remembered by different communities and each evangelist used the one he was accustomed to praying.

Taking Matthew's advice, we begin to reflect on the meaning of the words and phrases in the prayer. The first question we ask is whether Jesus was composing a new formula to replace the age-old formulas the pious Jews had recited for centuries. Or was he giving his disciples an example of the way they should structure their prayers?

The answer seems to be that he was doing both. It would be a good guess that Jesus meant his words to be used in somewhat the same way as he spoke them, as long as they came from the lips of his disciples with conviction and understanding, with faith, trust and love. But because of the danger that any formula too easily becomes so familiar that it is recited without thought or feeling, Jesus may well have meant his words to be a pattern, an example, of the sentiments his disciples should express in their own private prayers. As one author has said, the Our Father contains the great themes of our dialogue with God.

Matthew breaks in: "If you are to pray the Our Father from the depths of your hearts and be sustained by it each day, you need to reflect on the depth of meaning in each phrase. If you use it as a model for your other prayers, you need to understand its structure."

The structure is not too difficult. There is a greeting followed by seven petitions. The first three are "you" petitions, concerned with God. The last four are "us" petitions that are concerned with our needs.

We quietly say, "Our Father in heaven," and think that this is a simple enough greeting until we look at it word by word. What does that first word, *our*, convey to us? Is it merely an editorial plural or is it a true plural embracing others besides ourselves? Are we lone rangers, rugged individualists, standing in splendid isolation before the majesty of God?

The answer is a resounding no. Through Baptism we

have been united with Christ and with all believers into one Body. In every prayer we approach God arm in arm not only with Jesus but also with all other believers. By this word we commit ourselves daily to that all-encompassing love by which Jesus bound all believers to himself and to the Father. Those three letters spell out an act of faith. We assent not only to the ideals and values of Jesus but also to our intimate union with him and all his other friends.

We also find a wider meaning in that little word *our*. We realize that God is the Father of all people, believers or not. We are acknowledging the sovereignty of God over the entire human race and our solidarity with all human beings. This sense of the meaning of *our* has been experienced by many of the astronauts as they circled our planet. Many of them had a sense that the earth was a living organism. From space it was obvious that there was one air system and one water system encircling the earth. Rivers ran the length and breadth of the continents; there were no national borders.

Others had a profound spiritual sense that God had created one world and was Lord of all. Each person was a part of the much larger whole, the family of humankind. Each person was also a part of a larger network of relationships that encompassed all material things.

The word *our* we have said so many times connects us with God, with Jesus, with other believers and all people. It needs to be said slowly if its implications are to sink into our hearts and souls.

The word *Father*, like all other words, is lifeless in a spelling bee or printed on a page. It is our experience that enriches or distorts the word, that evokes good or bad feelings. Jesus clothed this word in great power and majesty when he used it as a metaphor for God. He chose it as the human word to describe the infinite God's way of relating to very finite people.

The prophets Hosea and Isaiah had spoken of God as

father, but that idea did not penetrate deeply into the minds and hearts of most of their hearers. The prevailing understanding of God stressed the divine transcendence, God's distance from the human. It emphasized power, law, justice and, to some degree, anger—along with love and care. This understanding of the Almighty led to such respect for God's name that pious Jews would not pronounce it. When they encountered the written name of God, they would substitute the word *Lord*. This practice created the word "Jehovah," which has no meaning in itself; it is composed of the consonants of *Yahweh* (the name of God) and the vowels of the word for "Lord," Adonai.

In this atmosphere of distance from the divine, of awe and majesty, Jesus spoke of God as Father. When he taught his disciples how to pray, he used the same word, spoken in the context of the care, love, protection, nurturing and gentle authority Jesus had experienced at home even when he caused his parents great worry.

When we use the word *father*, it may not always evoke warm feelings of being cared for, protected and loved. It may recall harsh treatment. Even the gender of the word may be disturbing. But when we unite with Jesus in praying these words, his sentiments become ours. We are not reaching our tiny frail arms out to a stern, judgmental male patriarch, but to a loving, caring Father who feeds the birds of the air, clothes the wild flowers in dazzling beauty and even keeps track of the very hairs on our head. This is a Father who says we need not worry about what we will eat, drink or wear because he will provide everything (6:31-34).

The nature of God can never be captured in a simple formula—not even in the most sublime and complex formulas. As soon as we say one thing about who God is, an opposing idea immediately presents itself. There always is, at best, a paradox if not a downright contradiction in our images of God. God is father. Yet, God is like a mother hen who gathers her young under her wings (23:37). Jesus tells us of a God who is so concerned about his flock that, like a good shepherd, he leaves the ninety-nine alone to find the one that is lost. He speaks of a God who is unrealistic in his generosity because he gives the same wage to the laborers who worked but one hour as he gives to those who worked all through the heat of the day (20:1-16).

Jesus conditions this loving, over-generous father-image: He is the "Father in heaven." In the ancient world, the one who had the highest seat had the most power. Placing God in heaven indicates that the Father has power over the entire universe. The God who resides in heaven is a God of power and might. He is a king who will punish those who reject his son (21:33-41); who will toss into outer darkness the one who does not come prepared for the wedding feast (22:1-14); who will send the Son of Man to judge the nations, calling some to inherit the Kingdom prepared for them from the beginning of the world but sending others into the everlasting punishment prepared for the devil and his angels (25:31-46).

We focus exclusively on one image of God to our peril. If we take the word *father* too narrowly, we have a male God and neglect the feminine aspects of God's care for us. If the judgmental God is our predominant image, fear will cause us to keep our distance from that stern judge. If our only image is that of the forgiving God, our own will may well replace the will of God in difficult situations. Images, contradictory as they may seem, reveal to us differing aspects of the God who is everything and everywhere.

As we muse over these first words in the prayer we begin to see that hidden in them is the key to developing the attitude basic to the first Beatitude: namely, a sense of our own weakness, littleness and poverty. The one who prays from the depths of his or her heart, "Our Father in heaven," is poor in spirit. Compared to the father, the little child is weak and dependent and needs help to get through the day. But the child also needs to realize that its father will not always protect it from the destructive folly of following its own will against the advice of its parents.

The next sentence, "Hallowed be your name," slips easily off our tongue. This is a slightly different translation than the one we were taught and still use at the Eucharist. *Thy* has been changed to *your*. Words get old and worn out. They pick up connotations that distort their meaning. *Thee, thou* and *thy* are such words. In our everyday speech we use *you* and *your*, forgetting that the other terms were once more intimate forms. Some English-speaking countries have made the change. Others, like the United States, have kept the old form in official prayers because they are familiar and because they have become an unofficial sacred language.

Other words for *hallowed* are *praise, bless, glorify*. The word comes from the Greek and means to set something apart for holy use, to make something holy. Certainly God's name is different, set apart from all other names. It is unique and holy. Therefore it is to be revered and respected. Moses handed down a specific commandment that God's name was not to be used in vain.

The word *name* has a much richer context in this prayer than we usually associate with it. For us *name* means simply to put a tag on someone or something to identify it and set it apart from other people or things. In ancient times, as among Native Americans, a name had a much richer meaning. It expressed some characteristic of a person. Thus the Hebrew name *Yahweh* apparently means, "He is who is," because when Moses asked God's name, the answer was, "I AM WHO I AM" (see Exodus 3:14). This name suggests that God is the one who is always present.

There is still a further difficulty with that short sentence. Is it merely a statement of the obvious fact that God is holy and present, in itself a very powerful and meaningful statement? Is it an acclamation of praise and

115

appreciation of the utter otherness and goodness of God, a joyful cry that God and God alone is holy? This is certainly an admirable exclamation. Is there a tone of the imperative in it? Are we asking God to make the name holy by bringing all people to acknowledge the divine holiness and rule over our lives? If so, we are asking that we experience God's holiness in our lives, that God will forgive us, change us, save us and make us more God-like.

Or, finally, is that sentence a command to *us* to make God's name holy and respected by all through the lives we lead and the efforts we make to bring others into a close union with God? If that is the meaning, certainly we are pledging to be pure of heart, merciful, thirsting for justice. God is glorified by the sentiments in our hearts and the actions that flow from them much more than from great buildings, beautiful art or powerful organizations. According to the psalmist it is not sacrifices and oblations, but a heart set on doing God's will and ears open to obedience that gives praise and glory to God (see Psalm 40:6-10).

All of these ideas are captured in the words, "hallowed be thy name." One or the other meaning will predominate in our intention if we utter them in more than a routine, rote manner.

We continue to reflect. The room is quiet. The temperature is right. The chair is comfortable. We relax and allow the words, "Your kingdom come," to percolate through our imagination. What images do they evoke in us? Do we see the Queen of England in her splendid ermine robes, opening Parliament or riding in a carriage surrounded by her Horse Guards? Do we see the pope in the popemobile waving to enthusiastic crowds? Perhaps we see the New York Stock Exchange where kings of finance are enthroned or dethroned by numbers racing across the big board.

What do we see when we use the word *kingdom*? Do we see people handing out soup and sandwiches to the men on skid row? Do we see eucharistic ministers hurrying to the homes of the sick? Do we see a church full of people singing while babies cry and toddlers squirm? Do we see the pope visiting Roman prisons? Do we see neighbors bringing a hot meal every evening to a mother exhausted from trying to care for newborn triplets?

God's Kingdom does have a king. Jesus has already described him not as a mighty ruler passing laws and riding in splendor among the populace, but as a father caring for his children. The Kingdom does have laws summed up in a great command to love God with one's whole mind heart and soul and to love others as we love ourselves. A king has to have subjects and the Kingdom of God has innumerable citizens: those who in faith pray "*Our* Father" and completely entrust themselves to God's love.

Why, then, can't this Kingdom be easy to spot in this world? The reason is simple: The reign of God's love in people's hearts is intangible. It can only be seen by its effects in people's lives. There is no one perfect image of what God's Kingdom is like.

Jesus was no better off than we are in trying to describe it. He used many parables to say that the Kingdom is like this or that, but always implying that it is not exactly the same as this or that. Kingdoms do not appear in history instantaneously and full blown. They grow slowly and gradually, like a mustard seed that takes time to become a sheltering bush or like a measure of leaven gradually working through the dough (see 13:31-33).

The Kingdom grows slowly in the hearts of people. It needs to be nourished with patience, forbearance and, especially, fidelity as the seed that has been sown in the heart germinates and grows. It is extremely difficult to know who actually belongs to the Kingdom. Only at its final revelation will it be possible to separate the good from the bad, the wheat from the weeds in the field or the useful from the useless in the net (see 13:36-43; 47-50).

The Kingdom is like seed that is sown and encounters difference types of soil as it lands (see 13:3-9). We can accept or reject it, nourish it or let it die from benign neglect. It calls for us to be single-minded, pure of heart in seeking it as we would seek a pearl of great value (see 13:45-46). The image we have of Kingdom directs the places we will look to see whether it is actually coming into being here and now.

What are we asking when we pray that God's Kingdom will come? Certainly we are looking forward to the final days when God's power and glory will be manifested and the everlasting reign will be established. That is a vision that does not stir up much enthusiasm in the hearts of many people. We would prefer to see God's Kingdom established on this earth, "an eternal and universal kingdom: a kingdom of truth and life, a kingdom of holiness and grace, a kingdom of justice, love and peace," as the Preface for the Feast of Christ the King describes it. We are asking that this Kingdom will be in our hearts, that we will enjoy the peace and all the other benefits promised to those who live by the Beatitudes. At the same time, we look for it to affect the structures of society, vastly changing the political, economic and moral dimension of human life in the world.

What do we hope will occur as we voice the wish, "Your will be done, on earth as it is in heaven?" We are praying that God's Kingdom will come! In typical Semitic fashion, the next petition repeats the previous one for emphasis.

As we consider this rephrasing, we first ask, what do the words *heaven* and *earth* mean? A legitimate question, but one that cannot be answered in a physical way. Heaven certainly is not up there in the cosmos where millions of galaxies race through space. It is within the heart of God. It is the mystery of the triune God, of Father loving the Son and the Holy Spirit, of the Son loving the

Father and the Holy Spirit, of the Holy Spirit loving Father and Son and of all three Persons loving human beings and all of creation. It is this perfect love relationship that we pray will be our lot and the lot of all those who do the will of the Father.

The earth is not just the mountains and the plains we cross, or the rivers and seas we sail upon. It is only partly the physical planet on which we live. Primarily it is the human heart which is created to love and sing God's praises.

The will of God is more than avoiding sin by keeping the commandments. It is a loving way of life characterized by humility, meekness, hunger for justice, mercy, single-mindedness and a certain amount of suffering. In other words, it is a life in which the Beatitudes have taken root and are growing. We cannot lay down a detailed plan of how each life is to be lived. Growing into the Beatitudes is a process that depends on the talents we have, the circumstances of our lives, the wisdom we have gained from life and the continued grace and call of God each day.

An important part of living within the will of God is the attitude we have as we pray the Lord's Prayer. Do we recite these words with dejected resignation, with a feeling that we can't escape what God has in store for us? Do we recite them in a bitter tone because we feel that life has dealt us a poor hand? Or do we recite them with anticipation and acceptance of what comes our way from the hands of a loving God? Each attitude will determine how we go about developing or stifling the attitudes of the Beatitudes.

A final question is whether we can hasten the time or the growth of the Kingdom here on earth. We do not bring about God's Kingdom even in our own lives. This is difficult to grasp because we are so used to taking charge of our lives. The coming of the Kingdom, in a mysterious way, depends on God and comes about in God's own time. We pray that God will hasten the time when the Kingdom will be firmly established in our lives and will embrace all people.

Yet even though the coming and the growth of the Kingdom does not in the last analysis depend on us, we do have a role in bringing it about. We can work at removing the self-centeredness that blocks the Kingdom's growth in our hearts. We can help improve the situations in people's lives that prevent them from embracing the Kingdom. It is hard to hear the gospel on an empty stomach or when one is flat broke, sick or in prison. We can prepare hurting hearts for the message of the gospel by removing some of the causes of those hurts. We can strive to cooperate with God's efforts by being living signs of what Kingdom life is like. To do all this, we need an attitude of dependence on God and a willingness to pay the price of helping.

FOR REFLECTION

1) *Quietly pray, "Our Father, who art in heaven, hallowed be thy name. Thy kingdom come. They will be done on earth as it is in heaven."*

   Quietly pray these thoughts a second time, but this time use your own words. What strikes you about these words?

2) *Over the years our predominant image of God will change. What changes have occurred in the way you picture God? How did you picture God when you were a child? How do you picture God now? What do you think caused you to change your image of God? How have these changes affected the way you relate to God?*

3) *What does the holiness of God mean to you?*

4) In what way do you see your ordinary daily life
  contributing to bringing about the Kingdom of God?

FOR PRAYER

Holy, holy, holy Lord, God of power and might,
heaven and earth are full of your glory.
Hosanna in the highest.
Blessed is he who comes in the name of the
  Lord.
Hosanna in the highest.

(Eucharistic Acclamation)

Chapter Fifteen

The Lord's Prayer, Part Two (6:11-14)

EVEN THOUGH THE TIME is getting short and he is anxious to leave, Matthew urges us to continue examining the petitions of the Lord's Prayer. We saw that the first part concentrates on praising God and expressing our hope that divine love will reign in the hearts of all people. Now we turn to our own needs. We are needy in so many ways and most of our private prayers are for help. Jesus gathered all the areas in which we need help into four petitions. If we reflect on the implications of each word in these requests, we will realize how much they encompass.

The first of these, "Give us today our daily bread," seems clear enough. *Give* simply means we are asking for a favor. We need help to get something or to do something that we cannot manage by ourselves. It is, in this case, an expression of our dependence on God for the most elemental things of life. It is another expression of how poor and dependent we need to become if the Kingdom of heaven is to be ours. As much as we would like to, we do not control the present and certainly not the future.

Coupled with this dependence is a note of hope, of trust. We do not ask people for help when we know that they cannot or will not give it. We ask for a favor from

123

someone who has power to do what we want and whom we trust will be willing to use that power on our behalf. That one word, *give*, is an entire prayer of trust and hope that flows from an attitude of total dependence.

The plural pronouns in this prayer are not merely polite ways of saying "me" and "my." They don't even extend our request for help to include our families and friends. Rather, those two words direct our sight to a world where two-thirds of the people go to bed hungry every night. It opens our eyes to those who are actually suffering, perhaps dying, from malnutrition. These two words are like clanging alarm bells that demand not only attention but also some type of response. They direct the request for bread in two directions. It wings its way in trust to the heart of the almighty and provident God. At the same time, it plunges back into our own hearts, rousing us to do what we can to provide for the needs of others. It reminds us that in part we are the answer to our own prayer.

Today and *daily* anchor us in the present. We are to have no undue concern about the future. This certainly is a difficult attitude to live by when our culture emphasizes providing for our old age, when estate planning is touted on all sides and insurance is a major business. Taken at face value, these two words have more impact on people who are actually worrying about what they will have to eat the next day.

All through history, a day laborer's daily pay put food on the table either that day or the next day. It was seldom sufficient for putting something aside for the day after next. Thus, if there was no work, there was no pay and not much chance to eat. For this reason, the Law of Moses commanded that a worker's pay should not be withheld at the end of a day. For the man standing on a street corner waiting to be picked up for a day's work in the fields or on a construction site, this request can be understood as asking for work so that he and his family can have bread on the table today.

But is the daily bread for which we ask merely food for the table? For those who are fairly secure in knowing where their next meal is coming from, it is also a request that things will continue to go well, that there be no natural disasters which would make it difficult to get food and that all their other needs such as health and peace be met. This request for daily food is also a reminder that we need to help feed those who do not know where their next meal is coming from. It is also a reminder that if people are going hungry very often, it is because of other people's greed. Gandhi put it well when he said that there is enough food for everyone's need, but not for everyone's greed.

It does not take a great amount of reflection to see a still deeper meaning in the bread we request. We ask for a daily allotment of the Bread of Life, Jesus, to sustain us on our life journey.

During the time when the Hebrews escaped from bondage and wandered in the desert for forty years, God gave them a daily measure of manna. It was a miraculous food that lasted for one day and only one day. In our struggle to escape the bondage of sin and to find the true promised land, our plea for food is as much a plea for spiritual nourishment as it is for physical nourishment. God offers Jesus to us each day as this nourishment.

Jesus is our daily bread in the words of Scripture, in the fellowship of believers and in the sacraments, especially the Eucharist. But we have to come to the banquet and eat what is offered in order for the miraculous food to nourish us. And when we have eaten, we must nourish others. We must become food for them by the care and love we extend to them. We become part of the daily bread given to them by a loving Father.

The different ways in which we understand this request will evoke different feelings as we pray it. For example, if we understand that petition to be merely a polite way of asking for food each day when we have the means to put food on the table, the request will slip off our tongues with a minimum of thought and without much sense of dependency. If, on the other hand, we are facing a crisis and have no one to turn to, this plea will have much more urgency. By reflecting on the petition word by word we can identify the disposition that should accompany our prayer.

Trusting in God to meet our daily needs is a challenge to our desire to control our own lives. It sounds foolish to our ears; it disturbs our peace of mind and is extremely difficult to put into practice day by day. Asking for food comes naturally enough, but the next petition, "Forgive us our debts as we forgive our debtors," goes against our grain.

We may wish to be forgiven, but we have a most difficult time in forgiving others. It is easy enough to identify the debts others owe us. We have been wronged, suffered injury, been mistreated. There are people on whom we would like to wreak revenge. There are people who owe us an apology or restitution in some form or other. There are people whom we do not want to forgive and people from whom we will not ask forgiveness.

But what is this debt that we are asking God to forgive? The more familiar translation of the words is "forgive us our sins." Again it usually is relatively easy to think of sins that we would want forgiven. But what about the times we say this prayer and we can't think of sins that need forgiving?

We are trying our best. We have not broken any of the commandments in a serious way. We have been steady, law-abiding, hardworking people. And so the first half of this petition prods us to become conscious of the good we could have done but did not do. It calls us to repentance for the times we have not been poor in spirit, or hungered and thirsted for justice, or made peace. It especially alerts us to situations when we have not been merciful and forgiving.

The second part of this request for forgiveness is a resolution that we will share in the Lord's work of reconciliation. Because we have been forgiven, we will forgive and befriend enemies. This work of reconciliation was manifested when Jesus told the man who was paralyzed and brought to him on a mat that his sins were forgiven. It reached its crowning point when Jesus on the cross forgave all those who had put him there. Every time we ask for forgiveness and every time we forgive we are extending that work of reconciliation.

That little word *as* that connects the first part of this petition with the second is not so easy to understand. Does it mean that God will forgive us only to the degree that we forgive others and that if we do not forgive others God will not forgive us? That's what 6:14-15 seems to say: "For if you forgive others their trespasses, your heavenly Father will also forgive you; but if you do not forgive others, neither will your Father forgive your trespasses."

How does this statement square with God's unconditional love? To be effective, forgiveness has to be accepted. By refusing to forgive others, we block our reception of God's forgiveness. We harden our hearts against Gods' love by refusing in return to give forgiveness to others. In effect, we say we will not become the kind of person God wants us to be.

God always allows us to be free, to choose the kind of person we want to be. God does not force us to forgive others and thereby show our love for God. In effect, we make it impossible for God to forgive us because we refuse to change and enter fully into the redeeming work of Christ. In refusing to do our part in bringing peace into the world, we refuse God's forgiveness as soon as it is offered.

Praying that we will be forgiven as we forgive is asking that the forgiveness given to us will not stop in us but will flow out to others, to those we have blacklisted for having injured us in some way. These words should not express fear of consequences, but a grateful pledge of how we will act when we have been hurt or rejected. It is an expression that our forgiveness will be as unconditional and as total as that of Jesus and his Father.

"Do not subject us to the final test" is a cry for help in the face of an overwhelming temptation that might lead us to turn our backs on God. No matter what the level of our understanding of this prayer or the fire of our spiritual life, we all face daily temptations. Some of these we can handle. Some seem so overwhelming that we need help in dealing with them. Some come from within and others assail us from the outside. Our inclination to do all things our way, to be self-seeking and self-centered, as well as the values of our culture try to steer us away from gospel values. Giving in to such temptations slows and even completely blocks our love relationship with God. Certainly the God who loves us is not going to seduce us, to push us, to lead us into temptation. What then does this petition mean?

It is not easy to express the meaning of Jesus' thought in modern English. A temptation is a test. It can lead to greater strength and holiness or it can lead to self-gratification and sin. In the garden on the night before he died, Jesus asked Peter to pray lest he undergo the test. Peter failed to pray and fell asleep (26:36-46). He then denied Jesus three times. In this sense the test can be seen as something so great that we can deny our faith if we are not prepared to seek God's help in prayer.

Which way we go depends on the choice we make. Just what are we asking for when we say this petition? It is unrealistic to think that we are asking God to remove all temptation from our lives. Our experience shows that this is not possible. Are we asking for help in those temptations against which we feel we have no defense? Are we asking for protection from one specific type of temptation? The various translations of this prayer in modern Bibles seem to imply different answers to this question.

The familiar translation is, "Lead us not into temptation." We could understand this as asking that we are never tested beyond our strength. New biblical translations vary: "And do not bring us to the time of trial" (*New Revised Standard Version*); "and do not put us to the test" (*Revised English Bible*); "do not subject us to the final test" (*New American Bible*).

All these translations seem to ask that we not succumb to the temptation that would totally and forever sever our ties with God. In other words, we beg for the strength and guidance of the Holy Spirit so that we will not be faced with an irrevocable choice between our will and God's will.

This ultimate hardening of the heart comes in subtle ways. We buy the illusion that what we physically experience is the ultimate reality and so do not see the reality of the spiritual. We get frozen into a formalism that holds onto the past because that is the way things have always been done. We do not expect God to work in different ways today. We want all people to act and think in the same way without honoring the uniqueness of each person and of each culture. The ultimate temptation comes camouflaged in many ways.

In a roundabout way, this petition harks back to the first Beatitude. The tests we face are whether or not we are willing to show our acceptance of God's gifts by being faithful to the norms and values of the gospel. The final or ultimate or greatest test will be different for each person. It can come at any time and in many forms. It will always be difficult, and we will always need the guidance and strength of the Holy Spirit to meet it.

One last word on this petition. It seems to be a petition that is focused on the individual, on "me." Yet it uses the plural, *us*. It is true that many of these tests are purely personal, but we also have to be concerned about those things that are a test or temptation for all of us.

Modern advertising, selfish economic theories, group prejudices, irresponsible TV shows test the commitment of all believers to the attitudes and values of Jesus.

This petition may then be seen as asking God to protect us from a lack of common purpose or from peer pressure that would lead the whole group to destruction by denying who we are as God's people. This has happened many times in history. It happened in Germany as Christians participated in the Holocaust. It is happening today in various parts of the world as Christians continue to participate in genocide and war.

"But rescue us from the evil one" seems too simple; we know what the verb means. We cannot overcome evil by ourselves. We need the intervention of another to spare us from a threatened disaster. It is as if we are being driven toward a precipice by a force we cannot stop and we call out for someone to rescue us. We feel that we are being chased by a roaring lion intent on devouring us or that some dark figure is attacking us. We need help.

The newer translations of this prayer substitute "the evil one" from the more generic "evil" of the older translations. Who is this evil one? It is the angel whom the Son of God saw falling from heaven. It is a powerful superhuman force defiant of and hateful toward God. It is Satan. We need help in dealing with the cunning attacks of the devil and his hosts.

But the devil has conducted a grand program of disinformation and a great many people do not believe that such a personal force of evil exists. Because of this unbelief, we are not on our guard against the evil one's wiles and snares. We are oblivious to the attractive traps laid for us. Our cry for deliverance is a plea that we become conscious of this evil power and that we be delivered from our blindness and our attraction to evil.

The devil and his cohorts are not the only evil ones whom we must fear. There is that most sinister evil one who looks at us from the mirror each morning as we wash up. This petition is a constant reminder that we are members of a fallen race. We are loved and we have been redeemed, but we are still full of self-centeredness, anger, lust, envy, sloth, greed and gluttony. Over the years we may have fostered attitudes and values that are contrary to the Beatitudes. The plea to be delivered is not a request for a magical changeover of our person, but for the knowledge, wisdom, love and strength we need to be peacemakers, to be merciful and forgiving, to feed the hungry and clothe the naked.

Evil is conquered only through good. The violence in our hearts is driven out only when it is recognized for the evil it is and when nonviolence, mercy and forgiveness take up residence. Greed is laid to rest by generosity, and so on. Deliverance from the evil one and from the evil in our hearts comes gradually as we take the nourishment offered us by the word of God and by the eucharistic bread, as we turn our hearts and actions over to Jesus more and more.

The evil from which we beg to be saved is not only the attacks and snares of Satan and of our own fallen nature. It is also that great avalanche of sin and iniquity rolling through the world. It is the accumulated effects of our own sins and the sins of all other people, including those who have gone before us.

When we hate someone, that feeling provokes reciprocal hatred and violence that gradually builds. The greed of the individual fosters greed in those who were despoiled. The sins of the parents may not be visited upon the children in divine judgment, but they usually are visited upon them by nature: The abused child becomes in turn an abusive parent.

The evil rolls on and on. Individually, we cannot stop this sweep of evil in the world, but we can stop the prejudice, the bigotry, the violence that has seeped into our own lives from our surroundings. We can unite with others to bring peace and justice and stem the tide of violence and injustice. In so doing, we are cooperating with God in delivering ourselves and others from evil.

Implicit in this petition is a request to God that our ears and hearts will be opened to the warnings of the prophets among us, who see clearly what God wants not only from us individually but also from us as a community, as a Church, as a nation.

These prophets are not always people obviously sent by God. In his speech at Gettysburg, Abraham Lincoln expressed ideals of justice for our nation that have inspired generations to struggle to secure human rights—a gospel value—for all people. This is a nation conceived in liberty and dedicated to the proposition that all are created equal. This is a nation under God. It has a government of the people, by the people and for the people. It is a nation that we hope will not perish from the earth. Each of these sentences addressed an evil, a false way of seeing what the United States is about. Each of these statements express a biblical view of what a nation can and should be.

The simplicity of the Our Father is deceptive. A child can utter it with trust and love, taking it at face value. A mystic can spend hours in contemplating the God who is addressed in these various petitions. A theologian can wrestle with the unexpected depth of meaning in the petitions, finding connections between them and the other great mysteries of the faith. An ancient writer, Tertullian, called it a summary of the entire gospel. In recent years outstanding theologians such as Bernard Häring and Romano Guardini have written short but profound books on it.

The Lord's Prayer is a way for everyone to navigate through life. The truths it contains are important, but the attitudes and characteristics it fosters are much more important.

1) *When you ask for daily bread, what needs usually come to your mind?*

2) *What connection do you see between forgiving and being forgiven by God?*

3) *What are some of the more subtle tests we face in our culture that tempt us to ignore God even though they do not cause us to deny God?*

4) *What are some specific indications that you have seen that there is a devil, an evil force, at large in the world?*

FOR PRAYER

Assign one petition from the Our Father to each person in the group to rephrase in his or her own words. Each person then recites his or her petition immediately after the leader recites the original petition. (Leader: "Our Father in heaven"; *member:* "God so far and yet so near.")

Conclusion

As Matthew prepares to take his leave and moves toward the door, we realize that we have only touched on some of the sayings in the Sermon on the Mount and that we have hardly looked at the events recorded in the narrative sections of his Gospel. We express our regrets that we have so little time to consider the rest of his inspiring book. He assures us that it was never meant to be read and discussed at one sitting. With a warm smile he encourages us to read it frequently on our own and to look especially for the connections between sayings and events, to discern the attitudes which these reveal and to compare our own lives, attitudes and practices with those we find in Jesus.

After he has said "Shalom!" and gone out the door, we once again review the Beatitudes. If we are honest with ourselves, we have to admit that, in purely human terms, they certainly are goals beyond our ability to achieve. We constantly have to struggle with the same temptations of pride, power and ease Jesus faced in the desert. We are frequently diverted from doing God's will in the present by the temptation to live in the past with its hurts, failures and unreal expectations or to live in the future, with its hopes of what might be or what could be.

A way to become conscious of these temptations working in our lives is to use the eight Beatitudes and the seven petitions of the Our Father, instead of the Ten Commandments, as the basis of our daily examination of conscience. Even though we do the best we can, we still need help. Prayer, fasting and almsgiving along with a sincere effort to put the will of God foremost in our intentions are the helps Jesus suggests. One thing is for sure. Matthew's Gospel is a message of encouragement and hope. The Lord did not die and rise to no avail. The help we need is available.

The words of Archbishop Oscar Romero are a fitting close to this effort to break open the Gospel of Matthew:

> It helps, now and then, to step back and take
>   the long view.
> The kingdom is not only beyond our efforts, it
>   is even beyond our vision.
> We accomplish in our lifetime only a tiny
>   fraction of the magnificent enterprise that is
>   the Lord's work. Nothing we do is complete,
>   which is another way of saying that the
>   kingdom always lies beyond us.

No statement says all that should be said.
No prayer fully expresses our faith.
No confession brings perfection.
No pastoral visit brings wholeness.
No program accomplishes the Church's
mission.
No set of goals and objectives includes
everything.
That is what we are about. We plant the seeds
that one day will grow. We water seeds
already planted, knowing that they hold
future promise. We lay foundations that will
need further development. We provide yeast
that produces effects far beyond our
capabilities. We cannot do everything and
there is a sense of liberation in realizing that.
This enables us to do something and to do it
well. It may be incomplete, but it is a
beginning, a step along the way, an
opportunity for the Lord's grace to enter and
do the rest.
We may never see the results, but that is the
difference between the master builder and the
worker. We are workers, not master builders,
ministers not messiahs.
We are prophets of a future that is not our own.

For Further Reading

To break open a Gospel, we need to read more than one commentary as well as the Gospel itself. The following volumes have contributed helpful insights to the authors.

Barclay, William. *The Gospel of Matthew*. The Daily Study Bible Series, rev. ed., Vol. 1. Philadelphia: Westminster Press, 1975.

Brown, Raymond E., S.S., et al., eds. *The New Jerome Biblical Commentary*. Englewood Cliffs, N.J.: Prentice Hall, 1990.

Crosby, Michael H., O.F.M. Cap. *Spirituality of the Beatitudes*. Maryknoll, N.Y.: Orbis Books, 1980.

Guardini, Romano. *The Lord's Prayer*. Manchester, N.H.: Sophia Institute Press, 1986.

Hare, Douglas R.A., *Matthew*. Interpretation, A Bible Commentary for Teaching and Preaching. Louisville, Ky.: John Knox Press, 1993.

Häring, Bernard, *Our Father*. Winona, Minn.: Saint Mary's Press, 1995.

The New American Bible. With the revised New Testament and the Revised Psalms. Available in many editions from various publishers.

Rohr, Richard, with John Bookser Feister. *Jesus' Plan for a New World: The Sermon on the Mount*. Cincinnati, Ohio: St. Anthony Messenger Press, 1995.

Trilling, Wolfgang. *The Gospel According to St. Matthew*. New Testament for Spiritual Reading, Vol. 1, ed. John L. McKenzie. New York: Crossroad, 1981.